CONTENTS

Introduction to the Third Edition
and
Acknowledgments

As well as including new items in the listings, a number of changes have been made to the presentation and arrangement of the contents. The introductory text has been expanded to include background information and examples which, it is hoped, will help those readers who may be unfamiliar with aspects of our railway history and records. For the convenience of users further categories have been separated out from the general lists as was done previously for shipping records.

The preparation of this edition has been possible only with the co-operation of many people. I am grateful to Richard Wood, until recently BR Records Officer, and two of his staff - Ian Coulson and Mark Pardoe - who have been supportive with information regarding material sent to nominated County Record Offices, for permission to quote from GWR Magazines and to use part of the GWR system map on page 99. County Archivists and Librarians throughout the country have been helpful in response to my enquiries, and I would like to thank Miss Claire Wright, a member of the staff of the Hampshire Record Office, whom I used as a sounding board for the views of a practising Archivist on the changes made. Her comments and those of her colleagues were most helpful. Dr. Frances Shaw at the Scottish Record Office and Dr. Roger Strong at the Northern Ireland Record Office have been generous in their support.

In particular I would like to thank Mrs. Alexandra Nicol, Head of Government Services at the Public Record Office, also Cliff Edwards, a member of her staff, for affording me their time and co-operation. The preservation of records for its own sake serves little purpose unless their existence is known and they are used. The aim of this book is to make the railway records known. The aim of the PRO is to make the organisation and access to the records "user-friendly", thereby encouraging their use. This is referred to in the text, and it is hoped this edition of the directory will help towards that objective.

T.R.

About the author

Joined the Great Western Railway in 1940 as a lad clerk at his home-town of St. Ives, Cornwall, and after working in the Operating and Planning departments retired in 1982 as a senior officer at the Paddington Headquarters of British Rail Western Region. The idea for this directory developed from the world-wide response to an offer to fellow members of the Cornwall Family History Society in 1986 to search GWR staff records which, at that time, were part of the Clinker Collection at Brunel University. Co-author with Charles Rudd, Assistant Librarian at Brunel, of *Japanese Railways in the Meiji Period, 1878-1912* published by Brunel University 1991.

WAS YOUR GRANDFATHER A RAILWAYMAN?

A Directory of records relating to staff
employed by railways in the following countries
with details of material and repositories

United Kingdom
Australia
Canada
Eire
India
New Zealand
South Africa
United States of America

THIRD EDITION

Compiled by
TOM RICHARDS

Published by
Tom Richards
and the
Federation of Family History Societies

Published by
Tom Richards and the
Federation of Family History Societies (Publications) Ltd
The Benson Room, Birmingham and Midland Institute
Margaret Street, Birmingham B3 3BS

First edition 1988
Second edition 1989, reprinted 1990, 1992
Third edition 1995, reprinted 1997

ISBN 1-86006-014-5

Copies obtainable from
FFHS (Publications) Ltd
2-4 Killer Street, Ramsbottom, Bury, Lancs BL0 9BZ
also available from
Tom Richards, 1 Apsley Road, Clifton, Bristol BS8 2SH

Printed and bound by the Alden Group, Oxford

ILLUSTRATIONS

Cover:

Great Western Railway Engineering Department staff at work converting the track from Isambard Kingdom Brunel's broad gauge (7ft 0¼in) to standard gauge (4ft 8½in) in the early hours of Saturday 21st May 1892, as part of the general gauge conversion in the West of England. A masterpiece of planning and execution, the whole of the GWR track from Exeter to Penzance was dealt with in that one weekend. The location is Saltash station on the Cornwall side of the Royal Albert bridge, designed and built by Brunel and opened in 1859, the year he died. The illustration first appeared in *The Graphic* and is reproduced by courtesy of Brunel University Clinker Collection.

Title page:

The locomotive is *North Star* which hauled the first GWR passenger train to run between Paddington and Maidenhead on 31st May 1838. Built for the 5ft. 6in. gauge New Orleans Railway of America, it was bought by the GWR, converted to Brunel's broad gauge and broken up in 1906. Members of the Firefly Trust are building a full size working broad gauge locomotive of the *Fire Fly* class, one of the most successful of the GWR broad gauge fleet, at the workshops of the Great Western Society at Didcot, Oxfordshire. For information apply to the author.

Page 18.

Memorial in Ely Cathedral to the driver and stoker (fireman) of a train on the Norfolk Railway who were killed in an accident near Thetford on 24th December 1845. See page 76. Information on the likely authorship of the verses is given in the 1968 Year Book of the Friends of the Cathedral. The illustration is reproduced with the kind permission of the Dean and postcards are available in the Cathedral shop. Railway disasters and the death of railwaymen in service, particularly in cases where they gave their lives to save those of passengers, have been the subject of a number of poems and ballads, both secular and spiritual.

Page 65.

The cover of the North Eastern Railway Magazine for April 1917. Company magazines were on sale to staff and the public at one penny. Some offered copies on high quality art paper at twopence as well as editions at twopence which gave insurance cover against accidents for one month.

Page 80.

In 1838 the railway authorities evidently relied on informers for information leading to prosecutions for theft of railway property. The reward of £7.10s.0d. must have been a considerable inducement bearing in mind the low level of wages.

Page 81.

One of the maps contained in the 1915 issue of the Railway Clearing House Book of Junction Diagrams. The lines owned by the various companies were identified by different colours.

Page 92.

Part of a U.S.A. Southern & Western Route advertisement 1854.

Page 101.

Handbill distributed by the N.U.R. in 1932 when the railway companies were proposing a wage cut of 10% across the board.

To Go On, is shewn by holding the **right arm** straight out, and pointing **across** the Rails, thus —, or by a **White Flag.**

To Go Slowly, is shewn by holding the **right arm** above the head, thus — or by a **Green Flag.**

Extract from GWR rule book 1865

INTRODUCTION TO THE RECORDS

1 *Historical background*

From the 1830's railways proliferated throughout Britain. They were not built to a great plan or design but piecemeal, and were financed not by the State but by private enterprise. Railways presented opportunities for the development of rural areas, and with their advantages over canals held out the prospects of substantial profits for speculators. With great enthusiasm lines were built, some in remote areas of the countryside, but, with no experience to go by, their prospectus in many cases was wildly optimistic. They did not all prosper, some being absorbed by larger companies or, due to financial problems, were forced into amalgamations or abandonment.

After the first world war it was realised that it was not economically feasible to perpetuate a national railway network with some 120 separate undertakings, and although nationalisation was an option, it was decided the best way forward was to group the undertakings in England, Scotland and Wales into four privately-owned companies. This was approved in the Railways Act of 1921, and 1923 saw the formation of the "big four" railway companies - Great Western, London Midland & Scottish, London & North Eastern, and Southern. The year 1923, therefore is referred to as the year of "the grouping" or "the amalgamation". These companies retained their identity until the end of 1947. On 1st January 1948 they were nationalised and became Regions of British Railways.

In the 1830's the Provost of Eton College opposed the building of the Great Western Railway as he feared the young gentlemen would use it to sample the delights and distractions of London. The Duke of Wellington, more forthright in his view of railways in general, said "Progress be damned. It will just enable the lower classes to move about and become discontented". Move about they certainly did and while the social effects are matters for the social historian, there was much to affect family historians.

Railways provided new employment opportunities, attracting men and their families to the larger centres of railway activity, and by the nature of the industry workers moved around the country to obtain promotion. In agricultural areas, where many families existed at bare subsistence level and employment was erratic, the arrival of the railway produced keen competition to secure employment in the new industry. In Cornwall, for instance, long before the railway from Plymouth to Truro was half finished in 1855, the Directors of the Cornwall Railway Company had received applications far outnumbering the total of staff they expected to employ, even though the level of wages had not at that time been decided. It was clearly the prospect of security of employment which was the attraction.

2 *The railway staff records*

The railway companies kept records of their staff, in varying degrees of sophistication, and it is not surprising that some have been lost in the many changes of office locations and re-organisations which have taken place over the past 150 years. What is surprising is that so much has survived, and for this we must thank the Registrars of the former companies, and in more recent times the work of the staff at the British Rail Record Centre and those of the Public Record Office, and, by no means least, those enlightened individuals who have rescued records from oblivion in rubbish skips and the buckets of bull-dozers and then made them available for use in a variety of repositories.

Staff records, of course, form only part of the extensive documentation involved in the setting up, operation and development of the railways. Custody of these records, some of which were required to be kept in perpetuity, was usually vested in the Company Secretary, and managed through a Registrar of Deeds and Records. The amalgamations of 1923 provided an opportunity for bringing records together under the four main line companies, but also, no doubt, resulted in some being lost or destroyed. A further merger took place following nationalisation, with the formation in 1953 of British Transport Historical Records under the control of the Secretary of the then British Transport Commission, the records being subsequently transferred to the Public Record Office on 1st April 1972.

The purpose of this book is to indicate for the benefit of family history researchers, records known to be available and where they are located, at repositories in the United Kingdom, and to increase public awareness of a national archive which is probably the most comprehensive of its kind in the world. Similar information is also included for a number of countries overseas.

An individual's railway career is recorded in his "service history" which includes full name, date of birth, date entered service, initial grade, place of employment and rate of pay. Applicants for appointment were required to submit their birth certificate, from which the register entries were made, so it is reasonable to assume that the entries are accurate. Subsequent promotions, transfers and wage increases are recorded, also offences, punishments and commendations. Awards for proficiency in railway related subjects such as first-aid and the ambulance movement are recorded, together with railway educational achievements and civic honours. Some registers even include information on an individual's employment before entering railway service.

The following is typical of the information in a service history and is in respect of my great-uncle. Each move was accompanied by a modest increase in pay, details of which are given. From the information it can be deduced, correctly, that he was born in the Liskeard area and died at St. Ives, giving a clue to the civil registration records involved, while the lengthy periods spent at Helston and St. Ives make a search of the electoral lists worthwhile to find out about places of residence.

GEORGE JAMES HARRIS	Reg No.28430	Born 12th September 1877
28 Oct 1899	Porter	Liskeard
25 Jan 1900	Porter	Penzance
1 Oct 1900	Porter	St. Ives
19 Feb 1912	Porter Guard	St. Ives
31 Mar 1915	Rail Motor Conductor	Plymouth
23 Jan 1918	Branch Guard	Helston
14 Jan 1929	Foreman	St. Ives
19 Jan 1942	Retired	

While some records, particularly for workshop staff, were kept on individual cards, most were maintained in large ledgers, usually one double page for each individual; on the left hand page were recorded the grades, promotions and rates of pay, the right hand page being used for offences, punishments, commendations etc. Some of the smaller companies, on the other hand, used books as small as a school exercise book. Staff registers may be indexed individually, while in other cases one index volume covers a series of registers.

The registers or lists containing this information form the core of knowledge available to the researcher but there are other sources available which provide background clues to assist the search. Membership records of superannuation funds, sickness benefit clubs and trade unions, records of personal accidents, apprenticeship, technical school and orphanage attendance give dates and details of occupation which can provide useful information.

3 *Identifying and finding the records you need*

Patience and perseverance are qualities well known to family historians but to trace a railway relative some basic information is required, without which it may prove impossible to trace an individual. I have been asked by a reader who knew only that an ancestor worked for a railway company, if I would "open my big book of knowledge" and tell all about him, on the assumption that I have transcribed the details of every man and woman who worked on the railways for the past 150 years. Alas, time is not on my side. It helps if you know, although not necessarily all at the same time, which company an ancestor worked for, the kind of job he had and approximate dates of joining or retiring from the railway. The name of a station or the area of the country in which he lived, together with a date, may be enough to start you off.

Registers list staff by departmental groups which have evolved over the years. Except for small companies whose whole establishment may be recorded in one book, each department maintained its own records, and it may be helpful to relate specific occupations to the departmental descriptions used by different companies.

Department	Occupation
Operating)	Staff concerned with operations, i.e. porters, shunters, guards,
Traffic)	signalmen, gatekeepers at level crossings, Traffic Inspectors,
Coaching)	and station staff generally.

Locomotive)	Engine drivers (enginemen), firemen (stokers),
Loco, Carriage and Wagon)	engine cleaners, labourers in loco depots, wagon repairers and examiners, loco workshop and carriage building staff, mechanical and electrical staff engaged in the maintenance of fixed and mobile plant e.g. lifts, mobile cranes, etc at stations and depots as well as in works and factories.

Commercial)	Staff engaged in the collection, delivery or handling of goods
Handling)	in freight depots, including horse and motor drivers.

Engineering	Staff engaged in the maintenance and renewal of the permanent way, bridges, structures and stations. Track maintenance staff sometimes described as surfacemen, platelayers or packers.

Signal)	Staff engaged in the installation, maintenance and renewal
Signal & Telegraph)	of signal boxes and signalling apparatus, telephone lines, telephone exchanges and telegraph equipment.

In addition miscellaneous groups cover Stores, Marine, Continental, Hotels and Catering, etc.

Management and clerical staff are generally recorded in separate registers from the wages staff and appear under their Departmental headings, such as Accountant's or Audit Office or by specific office, e.g. Headquarters, Divisional Superintendent or Secretary's Office, or simply as clerical staff. Salaried staff do, however, sometimes appear in registers which are predominantly wages staff .

In this directory records in the United Kingdom are listed under the name of the railway company and sub-listed under repository and class number in chronological order. Individual piece references are shown in square brackets after the item entry. Having found an item which is likely to contain the information you seek, together with its reference number and location, the address of the location and the facilities available for research are to be found in the locations section.

Records may be found in more than one register. Staff who worked for a company which was amalgamated into a larger one in 1923 may be in the registers of both. For example, Locomotive Department staff of the Brecon and Merthyr Tydfil Railway Company before 1923 are shown in the B&M registers listed on page 19. If they were among those taken over by the Great Western Railway in

1923 they should also appear in the Great Western Railway registers of late B&M Railway staff listed on page 30.

It should also be borne in mind that an individual can appear in more than one register within a company. Taking the Great Western Railway again as an example, a man who joined the service as a porter at Carmarthen, West Wales, would be shown initially in the Swansea Division Traffic Department registers. Any moves within the Swansea Division would be added to the original entry. If he then moved to, say, Swindon as a signalman his records would be transferred on a special form from Swansea to the Divisional Office at Bristol and entered in their registers. If he then had a further promotion to Paddington he would appear in the London Division registers which would then contain all his details. It is thus possible to work forward from the initial post at Carmarthen and backward from the final one at Paddington.

Records held by the Public Record Office which are listed in this directory show the letter code, class number and piece reference. The following example would be ordered as Rail (Letter Code) 23 (Class) 48 (Piece) :

> **Barry Railway**
> *Public Record Office (Rail 23)*
> 1883-1923 Reg of staff [48]

If you hold a reader's ticket for the PRO you can order up to three items in advance by post, by telephone or in person not later than 4.15pm for production on the following day. If you have never been there, a first visit can be a little daunting, and finding one's way through the system can be time-consuming. The Public Record Office are concerned that the facilities should be user-friendly and the system is straightforward once one gets used to it, but for the benefit of the first-time visitor, and with the approval of the PRO, a guide is included as **Appendix A**. Details of the computerised system for ordering items are given in **Appendix B**. It is hoped these will help those who have limited time at their disposal.

The staff at the Public Record Office cannot undertake research, but for individuals who cannot get to Kew, particularly those overseas, the Public Record Office will supply a list of Independent Researchers who will undertake research for a fee. Many County Record Offices now offer to undertake paid research. Enquiries as to charges and conditions should be addressed to the particular Record Office involved in your research.

At the Scottish Record Office pieces bear the prefix BR followed by a letter code for the railway concerned and class reference 15 or 4 e.g.

> **North British Railway**
> *Scottish Record Office [BR/NBR/15/]*
> 1885-1904 Dismissals Traffic dept. [57]

Items are ordered by completion of an order slip and in this case the reference would be BR/NBR/15/57. It should be noted that, except for the North British Railway, the Scottish Record Office does not hold many staff records. To avoid the risk of a wasted journey researchers should particularly take note of the need for prior notice of requirements, as many staff records are outstored. It should also be noted that the search room is at West Register House, a different location from General Register House, the address for correspondence.

4 *Staff magazines and journals*

A great deal of information can be found in the staff magazines of the various companies which contain a wealth of staff detail. The earliest staff magazine held by the Public Record Office is the Great Western Railway Magazine which ran from 1862 to 1864, but the Great Northern Railway produced the "Great Northern Journal" a couple of years or so earlier. The GWR brought out a new magazine in 1888, and this continued publication until 1947 when the GWR ceased to exist. The first issue in November 1888 named eight members of the staff who had retired or been transferred to other stations. References to staff activities increased steadily and 50 years later in an issue of 42 pages no less than 20 were devoted to staff changes and social activities.

These magazines, issued monthly, include reports of promotions, retirement presentations and obituaries, as well as social activities. Items of special interest were compiled by the editorial staff, but generally reports would be submitted for publication by the Station Master or an interested member of the local staff who usually acted as the distribution agent, and efforts were always made to find a photograph to accompany the report. Wartime issues carry letters and photographs from staff in the Forces, together with lists of those killed or wounded.

If a retirement date or date of death is known the staff magazines may be the best place to start a search. For example, in the case of George Harris, whose service history is given on page 3, if all we knew of his railway service is that he worked for the Great Western Railway and retired in 1942, a search of the 1942 volume of the GWR Magazine reveals the following in the April issue in the section "Among the Staff" and is accompanied by a photograph: -

"... Another West Country foreman, Mr. G.J. Harris, of St. Ives, has also received farewell gifts on retirement. At a function held on February 21st, Mr.N.W. Carbines, on behalf of local traders, made a presentation of a cheque, and Mr.R.P. Grenfell (station master) handed Mr. Harris a wallet of treasury notes with the good wishes of the staff. Both spoke highly of the excellent service rendered by the recipient and expressed the hope that good health and happiness would mark his retirement. Mr. Harris had spent 42 years in the service...".

This paragraph tells us that when he retired he was employed in the Traffic department in the Plymouth Division of the GWR and that he joined the service about 1900. It should be borne in mind that magazine reports relied on information supplied by local staff - some places were better at it than others - so it does not follow that every retirement or death will be reported in detail. Official information included in the magazines consisted of staff changes from one station to another and deaths of members of the various Superannuation and Provident Societies.

Staff magazines continued to be produced after nationalisation in 1948 as Regional monthly publications and subsequently combined in a newspaper style journal *Railnews*.

When staff went abroad it was not a case of "out of sight out of mind". Company loyalty died hard and many kept in touch with colleagues and events through the staff magazines. Many wrote to the Editor and the following example was printed in the GWR Magazine for November 1910:-

Dear Mr. Editor - Reading some GWR MAGAZINES received from a brother in the 'Old Country' brings back fond recollections, and the names and faces of some of my old workmates make one think of the old home. I first worked at Newport (High Street) Carriage Department, was moved to Swindon to learn carriage examiner's duty, transferred to Cardiff, from thence to Newport (Dock Street) and subsequently to Severn Tunnel Junction. I left the service of the good old company in 1903 and emigrated to the United States, where I worked on the New York, Chicago and St. Louis and on the Lakeshore and Michigan Southern railroads (both Vanderbilt systems). I then went west to Denver and worked on the Burlington route at the foot of the Rocky Mountains, going through the country to the panhandle of Texas, where I was employed on the Santa Fe railroad building a fence across the prairie to keep the bucking broncho and the long-horned Texas steer from getting on the track. This was a pretty wild country, the marshals or policemen carrying big Colt revolvers in their belts. Moving further south, I worked on the Cotton belt route (Gould system),and also the Southern Pacific railroad. Having travelled about 5,000 miles looking over the country, I returned to Ohio, where for the past two years I have worked for the City of Bellevue, and am doing very well. I enclose my photo for your up to-date magazine, and wishing it every success.

I remain,Yours truly, WILLIAM DAVIS "Ex-wheel-tapper", Bellevue, Ohio.

It should be borne in mind that formal records, such as directors' and committee minute books, include details of promotions at fairly senior level, staff accidents, gratuities and pensions. There is such a vast number of these records that it is not practicable to list in this directory details of the contents which would be of interest to family historians, but if one has the time and the patience to sift through those for the particular company involved they can provide information of value.

Apart from containing biographical information the railway staff magazines also provide interesting aspects of social attitudes before the advent of radio, television and instant reporting of events. Take for example the North Eastern Railway Magazine for April 1917. Today the events which were occurring then would be covered by television reporters in flak jackets, and the newspapers would be full of details of strategy and tactics. The NER Magazine devoted many of its pages to details of the careers and service of staff who were killed or wounded, or who had been awarded honours, but also found space for morale-boosting articles on the national food supply. Allotment cultivation, poultry-keeping, bee-keeping and how to manage a goat, were covered as well as a prize competition set up at the instance of Earl Grey for vegetables grown by occupiers of cottage gardens and allotments in the County of Northumberland. In the article on poultry-keeping it was interesting to read that before the outbreak of war the country had been largely dependent on eggs from Russia, Italy, Austria and Hungary, and the article on allotments promised further information on sweet peas and how to grow them for exhibition. A far cry indeed from the coverage of Bosnia or the Gulf War. There was much coverage of events designed to provide comforts for members of the staff serving at home and overseas. A dance was organised by lady members of the District Superintendent's Office, Middlesborough, to raise funds for parcels which contained: ¼lb. bomb bar cake tobacco, 200 Mansion House cigarettes, 3 oz. Mica mixture tobacco, 1 pipe, 2 tins Rowntree's peppermint gums, 1 12-oz. packet Horner's toffee, 1 shaving stick, 1 tin quinine and phosphorus tablets, 1 box melloids for the throat, 1 tin peppermints, 1 box Oxo cubes, 1 box tea tablets.

There is a wide range of newspapers and periodicals which cover many aspects of railway development and practice and some of these provide fruitful source material for the family historian. Among the professional railway journals *The Railway Gazette* carries a great deal of biographical information relating to staff above the rank of senior station master. At the turn of the century the journal, then known as *Transport and Railroad Gazette*, contained brief details of appointments and deaths. From 1909, as *The Railway Gazette*, and under the heading "Personal and Appointments", each issue contained the following detailed breakdown of the staff references in that particular issue: (a) Directorial changes; (b) Honours and Distinctions; (c) Obituary; (d) Promotions and appointments; (e) Retirements; (f) Presentations; (g) Social and miscellaneous; (h) Wills. This practice continued until 1913, from which date all these items were lumped together in one general index under "Personal". Copies of *The Railway Gazette* are to be found in many local reference libraries.

Another popular journal which carries biographical information is the *Railway Magazine*, which first appeared in 1897 and is still produced. This magazine is of particular interest for the interviews with General Managers and senior officers of many of the companies which lost their identity in 1923, as well as reports of promotions, obituaries and appointments to posts overseas.

5 *Aspects of railway employment*

Many repositories throughout the country have special collections of railway archive material, printed books and photographs which, while not necessarily including material directly related to railway family history research, can enhance one's knowledge of the conditions under which one's railway ancestors lived and worked. These are listed in the *Aslib Directory* and in *British Archives* (Foster and Sheppard), to be found in local Reference Libraries. Examples of these collections are the Clinker and the David Garnett Collections at Brunel University, West London (wide ranging but strong on Great Western Railway and printed books), the O'Dell Collection at King's College, Aberdeen University, (railways in Scotland) and the Ken Hoole Collection at the Ken Hoole Study Centre, Darlington (North Eastern Railway including constituents and successors). The Scottish Record Office has the A.G. Dunbar Collection (railways in Scotland) and the D.L. Smith Collection (Glasgow & South Western Railway). Researchers may have access to these by prior arrangement, and enquiries should be addressed to the location involved.

While we are concerned in this directory with the written and printed records of railway workers these alone will not convey the kind of life they experienced in a new and thrusting industry which had to learn as it went along. Many, especially locomotive staff, worked under conditions which today seem impossible to imagine, and any family history research involving railway workers will be enhanced by some knowledge of these conditions. Alfred Williams' book *Life in a Railway Factory*, (*London*, 1915) describes his experiences over 23 years in the GWR Works at Swindon. Frank McKenna's book *The Railway Workers 1840-1970* (*Faber and Faber* 1980) contains contemporaneous material, including the "double-home" turns of duty where driver, fireman and guard, who worked together as a team, spent half their time away from home in lodgings or hostels. In lighter vein *Memoirs of a Station Master* (*Adams & Dart* 1974), edited by Professor Jack Simmons from *Ernest Struggles* by Hubert A. Simmons (*Reading* 1879), is an entertaining, if at times irreverent, account of the author's life as clerk and Station Master on the Great Western Railway.

The information in the registers provides the bare bones of an individual's railway career, and for readers who may be unfamiliar with some of the terms and conditions under which railwaymen worked, it may be useful to know a little more of the background, and for examples reference will be made to conditions on the Cornwall Railway which opened from Plymouth to Truro in 1859 and extended to Falmouth four years later.

Before the advent of collective bargaining and trade unionism towards the end of the last century, while the Board of Trade laid down safety standards, each railway company set its own standards of employment, made its own conditions of service and paid wages on a scale fixed by itself. The more prosperous the railway, the more likely it would be that wage rates would be higher than those offered by a less prosperous undertaking, and a succession of bad years could result in arbitrary wage cuts.

The Cornwall Railway never paid a dividend on its ordinary capital, and when it did turn in some profit this was taken by the Great Western to repay debts to the Associated Companies without whose financial support the line would not have been built. Despite this the Cornwall Railway paid rates generally above the average. Salaries and wages were reviewed by the Directors once a year, and advanced by £5 or £10 a year for salaried staff, and one or two shillings a week for wages staff, depending on behaviour, increased responsibility and length of service. This procedure is reflected in a Cornwall Railway Establishment Report for 1874 (PRO *Rail 630/3*) in which the wages of the six passenger guards employed at Plymouth station were increased from 26 shillings to 27 shillings per week, an increase of some 4½%, with the comment "*These men have long hours of duty and only get their dinners at home one day a fortnight*". Such an enlightened management attitude was not universal, and may be explained in the case of the Cornwall Railway by the fact that the Directors were made up of Cornish gentry and businessmen rather than remote speculators.

Promotion from the lowest grade (porter) to shunter, guard and upwards to supervisor and Station Master, depended on ability and behaviour. Vacancies were not advertised. No man was forced to accept promotion if, for personal reasons, he preferred to retain his existing grade, but movement from one station to another, within a Division, without promotion, was an instruction and carried no appeal. Many men were perfectly happy to stay where they were, often in the locality in which they were born, for almost the whole of their working life. At St. Austell in Cornwall, there were three cases of men between 1865 and 1930 whose whole career was spent at that station, in two cases 46 years, the other 48.

Railway service frequently ran in families, with sons following fathers, especially in railway factories such as those at Swindon and Crewe. The GWR Magazine for October 1922 quotes an interesting example of four generations and a father following his son. William Sandrey was a schoolmaster at Gwinear in Cornwall until the age of 62, when he entered the service of the West Cornwall Railway in 1871. He was employed as a gatekeeper at Sandy Lane Level Crossing between Gwinear Road and Camborne stations, taken over by the Great Western Railway in 1878, and he remained at work until he was 84 when he retired on pension. His son, William junior, joined the West Cornwall Railway in 1870, and went to St. Ives as signalman on the opening of the St. Erth to St. Ives branch line in 1877. He remained there until he retired 34 years later. A son of William junior, Walter Sandrey, joined the GWR at the Company's Tregenna Castle Hotel at St. Ives in 1891, and Walter's son Vivian joined the GWR in 1920 as a fitter's apprentice at Plymouth.

Conditions of work were exacting and discipline necessarily strict. By its nature railway work involved individuals who, unlike workers in factories or shops, could not be directly supervised - train crews for example and signalmen at remote signal boxes. A disciplined workforce was essential, and for this reason ex-soldiers, particularly N.C.O's who were used to discipline, were welcomed as recruits to the railway service. A 12-hour day, often extending to 18 in the case of train crews, seven days a week, with no extra pay for overtime and Sunday work, was standard, but conditions varied between companies. The Cornwall Railway allowed one full rest day in every 14 days worked, without deduction of pay, on condition that the individual stayed at home, available for duty in emergency. They also allowed Station Masters and Booking Constables seven days annual holiday in the summer months, and all other staff three days in the year, in every case without loss of pay.

Discipline was strictly enforced. Trivial offences would attract a reprimand or "verbal caution". Slightly more serious offences would result in a fine deducted from wages, while serious offences would involve attendance before the Directors, with a hefty fine, loss of bonus, suspension from duty for a period or dismissal. Drunk on duty, theft of goods in transit, and insubordination were serious offences involving dismissal, although the individual had a right of appeal.

The earlier reference to "Booking Constable" may require clarification. From the earliest days men were employed as policemen, with civil police powers, to maintain law and order on railway property, especially among the thousands of workers engaged on railway construction. Before the introduction of the electric telegraph and the interlocking of points and signals they also patrolled sections of railway to ensure the lines were not obstructed and controlled the movement of trains by fixed and hand signals. The operation of points serving sidings and goods yards was undertaken by a separate grade known as Switchmen. With the coming of the electric telegraph and increased safety, the need to patrol the lines diminished, and their involvement with the operating department was further reduced by the concentration of signalling apparatus into lineside signal boxes with the creation of a new grade of staff known as Signalmen, but even up to recent years the Signalman has been known familiarly, particularly by train crews, as "the bobby".

Because they had more time available due to the change in their duties, many Constables were able to undertake clerical work, including the issue, or "booking" of tickets, and these men were upgraded as Booking Constables at a higher rate of pay. In many cases they assisted the Station Master with clerical duties, while at smaller country stations they would be in sole charge.

The Duke of Wellington's forebodings about the movement of the lower classes were to some extent justified by the use of railways by criminals and theft of goods in transit. In 1853 the Goods Manager at Euston wrote: "...*Thieves are pilfering the goods from our wagons to an impudent extent. Not a night passes without wine hampers, silk parcels, drapers boxes or other provisions being robbed...*". As a result the policeman's duties turned increasingly to crime prevention and detection. Prior to the amalgamation of 1923 the various companies had their own police establishments. With the creation of the four main line companies these were amalgamated into four police forces, and following nationalisation a unified force was created, now known as The British Transport Police.

The Rules and Regulations applicable to police officers of the Stockton & Darlington Railway in 1846 were comprehensive. Their hours were from six o'clock in the morning until eight o'clock in the evening, with one hour for dinner, and half-an-hour for breakfast and tea, each. They had to prevent, as far as possible, all walking on the railway, any spare time between the arrival and departure of the trains being spent on the line where most needful. They had to report any enginemen stopping at public houses, or otherwise neglecting their duty, and they also had to watch the speed of trains. To assist them a table was provided showing the rate of travelling based on the time taken to cover a quarter of a mile. The S&DR management evidently wished to cover all contingencies as the speeds ranged from one mile per hour to 900!

6 *Social and educational*

Although railway work was hard and exacting, in many cases the railway proprietors displayed a paternalistic concern for the welfare and education of their employees, probably because it was in their interests to do so. Staff had to live within easy reach of their places of work, and railway houses were provided at widely different locations, ranging from a single cottage for a surfaceman at the lineside on a remote section of the West Highland line to towns such as Swindon, Crewe and Wolverton where workshops were established. These towns owe their origin to the growth of the railway industry, as in addition to artisan dwellings the companies built schools, hospitals, churches and orphanages. As time went on, the companies encouraged Staff Housing Associations with modest mortgages. Many of the original railway housing estates have disappeared as a result of social changes and redevelopment. One major exception is the estate adjoining the site of the former Great Western Railway locomotive works at Swindon. Restored and still used as dwellings in a conservation area, these buildings are a reminder of the part played by the railway in the development of the town.

Assistance for staff facing domestic difficulties was provided by the Railway Benevolent Fund and voluntary organisations such as the Great Western Railway "Helping Hand" Fund. Convalescent homes, funded by staff weekly contributions and supported by Management, are still in use.

The locomotive, carriage and wagon works of the companies called for large numbers of technically competent staff, and technical schools built and managed by the companies played a vital part in the training of the workforce. Apprenticeships were offered and many young men trained in the schools and the railway workshops went on to become some of the most innovative and respected locomotive designers in the world. Study was not a soft option and the GWR New Swindon Mechanics' Institution syllabus of the Science and Art Classes for the

October 1888-May 1889 session would not be amiss in any present-day technical course:

> *Geometrical drawing (elementary stage), practical plane and solid geometry, machine construction and drawing (elementary and advanced), building construction, arithmetic and mensuration, mathematics, theoretical mechanics, applied mechanics, steam and the steam engine, freehand and model drawing, geometry and perspective, carriage building; sound, light and heat; magnetism and electricity, and inorganic chemistry.*

Education of their employees was not confined to technical apprenticeships. Courses covering subjects such as station accountancy, goods station working, safe working of railways (rules and regulations) and salesmanship were held at main centres, and those members of staff who could not attend were encouraged to learn through correspondence courses, culminating in written examinations. Locomotive department staff joined "Mutual Improvement Classes" where they acquired knowledge of the techniques of driving and maintaining steam locomotives. The very fact that an individual was prepared to spend time on study was important when it came to selection for promotion, and in some grades achievement in the educational courses was essential for advancement. Local rivalry among staff for the highest marks was intense, especially as exam results were published in the staff magazine.

It was not entirely a case of all work and no play. As well as the annual office outing, staff were encouraged to engage in a multiplicity of social activities. These ranged from athletics, darts, chess and other indoor activities to choral and dramatic societies, "Fur and Feather" societies, music festivals and exhibitions.

With the active support of the management Staff Associations were created at many stations where staff could meet together socially. All these various pursuits were reported in the staff magazines. There were also occasions when staff had to act as social workers, as shown in the following report in the June 1914 issue of the GWR Magazine:

> *A problem giving rise to some anxiety had to be faced recently by the officials at Cardiff station. A little girl about 4 years of age, arrived there from Devonport unaccompanied, with a label attached to her frock giving an address in Cardiff. With kindly consideration Foreman Davis provided a porter to take her to the address shown, but the people there declined to take her in and she had to be taken back to the station. Inspector W. Cullen thereupon arranged for her to be fed, washed, and made comfortable by the waiting room attendant, and started a collection among his colleagues to add to her contentment. The police were informed of the circumstances, and they decided to have her looked after at the workhouse until her parents, who were at once communicated with, arrived a day or two later to take her back home.*

Obviously not a case of "Home Alone", but rather "Lone Voyager".

7 *The Railway Clearing House*

Although it was not a "Railway Department" as such, the Railway Clearing House played a vital role in the functioning of Britain's railways prior to nationalisation. Lack of standardisation in the early days produced major problems and it was realised that as the links between the emerging companies extended and through passenger train services became a reality, through ticketing would be needed, requiring standard tickets and a system of apportioning the revenue. One problem was solved by Thomas Edmonson, a former booking clerk on the Newcastle and Carlisle Railway, who designed card tickets and printing machines which produced a standard form of ticket. The other problem, how to divide the revenue, was solved by the creation of the Railway Clearing House which apportioned the amount due to each Company on the basis of the mileage covered. The same system applied to goods and parcels which could be despatched to any place where they could be handled.

Nine companies in the Midlands and the North signed up in 1842 and gradually the rest of the companies joined. The Clearing House, known to railway staff as the RCH, was based in London and at its peak as many as 2,500 clerks were employed, many of whom were recruited from the railway companies. A similar organisation was set up in Ireland. The ability of the RCH to apportion revenue on a mileage basis meant that through ticketing from, say, the West of England to the North of Scotland was no problem, even from small stations. Railway maps were produced for the Clearing House by Zachary Macaulay and at a later date books of Junction Diagrams, giving detailed distances between points where company lines met, were produced by John Airey.

Following nationalisation the RCH was no longer required for its original purpose, and was officially dissolved on 8th April 1955. However, it continued to perform a number of functions after this date and was finally disbanded on 31st March 1963. We have a legacy in the form of the superb railway maps of Zachary Macaulay and the junction diagrams of John Airey, and a fine collection of these is to be found in the David Garnett Collection at Brunel University, West London.

8 *Railway contractors*

While railway proprietors provided the funds for building railways, the actual construction was undertaken by contractors, some of whom, such as Brassey, Peto and Mackenzie, became world leaders in the profession. As the staff were employed by the contractor and not by the railway company, they do not appear in railway records. Some contractors kept records of their senior and specialised staff who stayed with them and moved from one contract to another, but no records were kept of the itinerant labourers. In many cases men who worked on building a railway left the employment of the Contractor on completion and joined the staff of the Railway Company, mainly as engine drivers or track maintenance staff.

Information on railway contractors is outwith the scope of this directory, but a detailed study has been undertaken by Lawrence Popplewell. Information regarding the various railway contractors and the work they undertook on railways in the UK is to be found in his series of ten gazetteers of railway contractors and engineers, covering all regions of Britain and Ireland (also two for Australia), all published by Melledgen Press, 71 Thornbury Road, Southbourne, Bournemouth BH6 4HU.

9 Railwaymen abroad

Researching one's railway ancestors in Britain is one thing; trying to find those who went overseas can be more difficult. The rapid rate of development of railways in the UK attracted speculators abroad to do the same, and men with experience, who worked on railways in this country, were much in demand, not only as artisans in their own right but also as instructors for local staff. Engine drivers in particular were much sought after. Some men went in response to advertisements, particularly by the Crown Agents for the Colonies, others at the suggestion or recommendation of friends and colleagues who had preceded them.

In 1850 a strike on the North British Railway in Scotland resulted in the following item in the Illustrated London News issue for June 15; *"North British Railway drivers unable to agree with management terms decided to emigrate to U.S.A. with funds contributed by drivers of other lines"*. In the I.L.N. issue for November 9 1850 the following item appeared: *"A great number of hands recently employed by the Eastern Counties Railway Company at Stratford emigrated to America, where it is said there is a demand for various classes of mechanics connected with railway works at higher prices than in England"*. Another item appeared in the Illustrated London News for June 24 1854; *"Several of the oldest drivers on the Manchester Sheffield and Lincolnshire Railway are leaving their situations and going to India. The inducement is the high rate of wages offered"*.

An early example of direct recruitment, on a temporary basis, is given in the Great Western Railway Magazine for March 1901 by a Great Western clerk, one of ten from Paddington, Bristol, Bath, Chester, Tiverton, Exeter and Stourbridge Junction, who were sent with 30 clerks from other companies to South Africa following an urgent request to the Prime Minister for experienced clerks to fill posts on the railways in the Orange River Colony and the Transvaal vacated by Dutch employees of the Netherlands Railways. He recounts their experiences among the Boer refugees on their journey from Capetown to Johannesburg. How they were dispersed between Johannesburg, Bloemfontein, Klerksdorp, Volksrust and other stations, and while they had no regrets at going it is clear they missed the Old Country. Tiverton to the Transvaal must have been a remarkable experience.

The GWR Magazine for November 1936 gives an indication of the kind of appointments taken up abroad. A senior officer in the Chief Goods Manager's Office at Paddington was appointed Deputy General Manager of H.E.H. The

Nizam of Hyderabad's State Railway; a member of the staff of the District Goods Manager at Reading, who had previously left to become Assistant Secretary, Takoradi Harbour, Gold Coast Government Railways, was promoted to Traffic Manager of the same railway, and a member of the clerical staff at Kidlington station resigned to become a Station Master on the Tanganyika Government Railways. An unusual overseas appointment was reported in the GWR Magazine for December 1945. Mr. F.J. Burrows, of the Traffic Department, Ross-on-Wye, at one time President of the National Union of Railwaymen, was appointed Governor of Bengal, with administrative responsibility for a province with a population of some sixty million. A far cry from the Forest of Dean.

Railway staff of all grades went from the UK to many countries, from Chile to Alaska, Africa to Japan, but the records listed in this directory cover only a small number of countries overseas. The countries included are those which were most easily researched, but even so the response to the initial questionnaires was patchy. The greatest disappointment was the U.S.A. Very few undertakings replied and only the Union Pacific Railroad agreed to provide information for inclusion. The railroads played a vital part in opening up the American west and it seems that a large slice of that continent's historical heritage has been lost. It is understood, however, that Railway Historical Societies in the U.S.A. are playing a role in trying to track down early documents, and any information on the whereabouts of staff records there will be welcomed.

Many senior staff who went abroad appear in the personal columns of *The Railway Gazette*. Those who went as engine drivers, clerks, engineering staff, storekeepers etc are more difficult to track down, but efforts are still being made to locate records in countries abroad, particularly South America and Japan. With the generous co-operation of a correspondent resident in Cape Town information is included on sources for South African railway records and it is hoped that further enquiries will provide information for other African states.

10 *Further reading*

Hundreds of books and pamphlets have been written on the history and development of railways in Britain. These are listed in "*A bibliography of British railway history*" by George Ottley, published by HMSO. Some have already been mentioned in the text. For anyone unfamiliar with the complexities of railway geography prior to the amalgamations of 1923 Ian Allan's "*Pre-grouping atlas and gazetteer*" (1983) and Alan Jowett's "*Railway Atlas of Great Britain and Ireland*" (1989) will be found essential aids. "*Victorian Railwaymen*" by P.W. Kingsford deals admirably with the staff as people. Railway housing and the development of the Estate and Property departments of UK railways are covered in depth in "*The Railway Surveyor*" by Gordon Biddle. Philip Bagwell's book "*The Railway Clearing House in the British Economy 1842-1922*" describes the development and the work of the RCH, and information on Zachary Macaulay and John Airey is contained in *"Railway Maps and the Railway Clearing House. The David Garnett Collection in Brunel University Library"* published by Brunel University in 1986.

11 *End-note*

The compilation of an index of individual railway staff would be an impossible task. Apart from the sheer volume of numbers, records have been lost or destroyed in the many absorptions, amalgamations and reorganisations which have involved the railways since their early days, but it is hoped this third edition of the directory will help more researchers to find their way around those records which survive. For the same reason it is not possible to claim that this is a definitive directory of railway staff archives. Material exists which has yet to be processed. It is possible that more records have yet to be discovered, and there is always the hope that others which at present may be in private collections will eventually find their way into public repositories, or in some way be made available for public research.

I would like to make it clear that while the Public Record Office, the Scottish and Northern Ireland Record Offices and other repositories have generously made available to me information on their holdings, the extraction of the details in this directory from their indexes has been done by me. Any errors in the text are entirely my responsibility and I would appreciate my attention being drawn to them.

ERRATUM
*Page 53. Southern Railway item Rail 651/131 should be **Rail 648/131.***

IN MEMORY OF

WILLIAM PICKERING,

who died Dec.R 24. 1845
AGED 30 YEARS

ALSO RICHARD EDGER

who died Dec.R 24. 1845.
AGED 24 YEARS.

THE SPIRITUAL RAILWAY

The Line to heaven by Christ was made
With heavenly truth the Rails are laid,
From Earth to Heaven the Line extends.
To Life Eternal where it ends
Repentance is the Station then
Where Passengers are taken in
No Fee for them is there to pay
For Jesus is himself the way
God's Word is the first Engineer
It points the way to Heaven so dear.
Through tunnels dark and dreary here
It does the way to Glory steer.
God's Love the Fire, his Truth the Steam,
Which drives the Engine and the Train,
All you who would to Glory ride,
Must come to Christ, in him abide
In First and Second, and Third Class,
Repentance, Faith and Holiness.
You must the way to Glory gain
Or you with Christ will not remain
Come then poor Sinners, now's the time
At any Station on the Line.
If you'll repent and turn from sin
The Train will stop and take you in.

Ely Cathedral,
Tombstone in South Porch

RECORDS AND DOCUMENTS FOR RAILWAYS IN ENGLAND, SCOTLAND AND WALES

Two important dates to remember:
1923 Amalgamation into four major companies
1948 Nationalisation into five Regions of British Railways
The following entries include brief historical information pre-1923

ALEXANDRA [NEWPORT & SOUTH WALES] DOCK & RAILWAY
Incorp 1865
Public Record Office
See GWR amalg lines regs, pp 29 and 30

ASHBY & NUNEATON JUNCTION RAILWAY
Incorp 1867. To L&NW/Mid Jt. Cttee 1893
Public Record Office [Rail 410]
1902-1910 Tffc, police and telegraph depts [1801]

BARRY RAILWAY
Incorp 1884
Public Record Office [Rail 23]
1883-1923 Reg of staff [48]
1886-1922 Reg of clerical staff [46]
1888-1922 Reg of loco drivers [49]
1888-1921 Reg of loco firemen [50+51]
1890-1923 Reg of stores staff [47]
See GWR amalg lines regs pp 30 and 31

BIRKENHEAD RAILWAY
Chester & B'head Rly incorp 1837. Vested in B'head, Lancashire & Cheshire Jcn Rly 1847. Name changed to B'head Rly 1859. Vested in GW and L&NW jointly 1861.
Public Record Office [Rail 35]
14.4.1848 List of working staff and amount paid per annum on Birkenhead Lancashire & Cheshire Junction Railway [38]
Nov. 1848 Pay Bill for Loco & Carr.Dept [39]
9.3.1850 Report from Engr (W.Bragg) with staff lists [24/3]
24.3.1852 Report from Engr (G.Douglas) with staff lists in Loco, Carriage & PerWay depts [24/5]
Mar.1852 Lists of working staff [45]
Oct.1856 Lists of working staff [46]

BIRKENHEAD RAILWAY (Cont)
Public Record Office (Rail 35) (Cont)
June 1858 Subscription list for widow of Thomas Stratford, gatekeeper at Birkenhead [48]

BLYTH & TYNE RAILWAY
Incorp 1852
Public Record Office [Rail 56]
1853-1856 Agenda book, Directors' meetings, inc details of housing and staff [6]

BRANDLING JUNCTION RAILWAY
Incorp 1836. To Newcastle & Darlington Jcn 1845
Public Record Office [Rail 64]
1839-1843 Reports re construction etc inc staff list [8]

BRECON & MERTHYR TYDFIL JUNCTION RAILWAY
Incorp 1859
Public Record Office [Rail 65]
Registers of appointments, retirements and dismissals
1880-1888 Permanent Way staff [31]
1880-1888 Locomotive staff [32]
1880-1888 Station staff [33]

See also GWR amalg lines page 30

BRITISH RAILWAYS [EASTERN REGION]
Northamptonshire Record Office
1947-1965 Woodford Halse staff rosters [ZA 9972]
c1960-1964 Woodford Halse Nat. Ins. stamp issues [ZA 362]
?1960's Woodford Halse guards permanent roster [164]
1965 Woodford Halse guards relief rosters [162/1-7]
1965 Woodford Halse shunting staff roster [163]

BRITISH RAILWAYS [SCOTTISH REGION]
Scottish Record Office [BR/RSR/15]
1947-1955 Regs salaried posts, Edinburgh Dist [256-260]
1948-1964 A.S.E. files for:
Aberdeen District Sal & Optg
Burntisland District Optg
Dundee District Wages & Optg
Edinburgh Dist Optg & various [254]
1953-1954 Regs wages staff, Edinburgh District [266-270]
1958-1959 Weekly staff changes, Optg Dept Edinburgh District [271]
1960 Stn Masters,Edinburgh Dist [272]
1969 Reg salaried posts, East Coast Division [273-275]

Scottish Record Office
A G Dunbar Collection [GD344]
1901 and c1952 Staff book Dawsholm shed includes **Cal Rly** [5/19]
1910-1957 Seniority list Yoker shed includes **Cal Rly** and **LMS** [2/39]

BURTON AND ASHBY LIGHT RAILWAY
Public Record Office [Rail 491]
1906-1920 Staff register [1038]

CALEDONIAN RAILWAY
Incorp 1845
Scottish Record Office [BR/CAL/4]
1888 Letter appointing William Stewart porter at Larbert [262]
May 1889 *The Baillie* periodical with note on G.Graham, Ch.Eng [211]

Scottish Record Office [BR/CAL/15]
1848-1919 Reg Optg dep Northern Sec [8]
1854-1877 Reg Engineering Works [22]
1867-1926 Reg Aberdeen Jnt pass stn [6]
1876-1931 Reg Dundee-Aberdeen Dists [1-3]
1877-1925 Reg Goods dep Northern Sec [7]
1881-1930 Reg St.Rollox Works [20 + 21]
1884-1926 Reg CR & NBR Jnt Aberdeen [5]
1888-1919 Adv. wages, trimmers [25]
1889-1897 Reg Engineering Works [23]
1892-1932 Individual histories (17)
1901 Tffc dep staff, hours etc [9]

CALEDONIAN RAILWAY (CONT)
Scottish Record Office (BR/CAL/15) (Cont)
1904 Tffc dep staff, hours etc [10]
1904-1920 Staff, pay etc [14]
1907 Tffc dep staff, hours etc [11]
1914-1922 Reg,Engineering Works [24]
1914-1916 Reg, DTS Aberdeen [4]
1917-1925 Testimonials, staff leaving St. Rollox [26]
1919-1935 Reg, Dawsholm loco depot [12]
1920-1923 Staff, pay etc [15]
1921-1923 Reg, clerks attendance Transfer Dept [18]
1923 Casualties and offences [16]

Scottish Record Office
A G Dunbar Collection [GD344]
1870-1931 Staff book Balornock shed includes **LMS** [2/38]
1888 Perth General stn paybill [1/84]
1890 Perth General stn paybills [1/99]
1901 and c1952 Staff book Dawsholm shed, includes **BR(ScR)** [5/19]
1910-1957 Staff seniority list Yoker shed, **LMS** and **BR(ScR)** [2/39]
1922-1926 Staff book Polmadie shed, includes **LMS** [2/46]

CAMBRIAN RAILWAYS
Incorp 1864 by dissolution of four railways in Mid-Wales. Further amalgamations 1865 and 1904.
Cheshire Record Office [NPR2/]
1860's-1900's Tffc dept salaried and wages staff [25]
1870's-1950's Originally **Cambrian**, latterly **GW**.Tffc dept salaried and wages. Includes Cambrian GM, Secretary and Accountant, and GW D.T.S. Oswestry [26]
1890's-1900's GM's Office staff included in **GW** reg for Central Wales District [22]
c1890-1945 Reg Tffc dept staff. Includes **GW** Central Wales Dist staff [27]
N.D. Index to unidentified Tffc dept reg. Mostly wages staff but some salaried. Includes **GWR** entries for DTSO Oswestry [9]

CAMBRIAN RAILWAY (Cont)
Public Record Office [Rail 92]
c1870-1922 Reg, Goods dep outdoor
[145]
c1870-1922 Reg, uniformed stn staff
[146]
1892 John Hood, dismissal [140]
1898-1922 Reg, Loco dep [142]
1904-1913 Reg, proms & tfrs [144]
1915-1944 Tffc dep medical exams [143]
See GWR amalg lines pages 30 and 31

CARDIFF RAILWAY
Docks and railways at Cardiff were
transferred from the Marquis of Bute
to Cardiff Docks & Railways in 1886.
Changed to Cardiff Railway 1897.
Public Record Office [Rail 97]
1810-1922 Reg, Engineering dep [32]
1867-1922 Reg, general staff [35 + 36]
1870-1922 Reg, supervisors [34]
1871-1922 Reg, clerks [33]

Public Record Office [Rail 1057]
1913 Henry Ree, Ch Engr, resignation
[1381]

CARDIFF BUTE DOCK
Public Record Office
See GWR amalg lines page 30

CARDIFF GAS WORKS
Public Record Office
See GWR amalg lines page 30

**CARMARTHEN AND CARDIGAN
RAILWAY**
Incorp 1854. Amalg with GWR 1881.
Public Record Office [Rail 99]
1869 Wages lists, Loco, Tfc, PWay deps
[57]
1870, 1874, 1875 Wages lists [58-60]

CHESHIRE LINES COMMITTEE
Public Record Office [Rail 110]
1907-1916 Super. Fund declarations
[161]
1915-1926 Staff irregularities [160]

CHESTER AND HOLYHEAD RAILWAY
Incorp 1844. Worked by L&NW from
1856.
Cheshire Record Office [NPR/2]
c1875-1905 Staff reg. [10]

CHESTER & HOLYHEAD RAILWAY (Cont)
Cheshire Record Office (NPR2/) (Cont)
c1890-1913 Staff reg [11]
May 1908 Goods staff at Holyhead [12]

Public Record Office [Rail 113]
See L&NW Rly [1862] page 37

**CLEATOR AND WORKINGTON JCN
RAILWAY**
Incorp 1876. Worked by Joint Committee
with Furness Rly from 1877.
Public Record Office [Rail 119]
1879-1923 Reg, Tffc Dept [13]

**CLEOBURY MORTIMER & DITTON
PRIORS LIGHT RAILWAY**
Auth 1901
Public Record Office [Rail 1057]
1908-1919 Staff correspondence [410]

**COCKERMOUTH KESWICK AND PENRITH
RAILWAY**
Incorp 1861. To L&NW/NE 1863
Cumbria Record Office
1878-1904 Keswick stn records, inc Mr.
P. Thompson, Stn Master [DX/1115
+1127]

CORNWALL RAILWAY
Incorp 1846. Leased to GWR, Bristol &
Exeter and South Devon from 1859.
Amalg with GWR 1889.
Cornwall Record Office
Transcripts of PRO items *Rail 630(2 + 3)
See below.*

Devon Record Office
Transcripts of PRO items *Rail 630(2 + 3)
See below.*

Public Record Office [Rail 134]
1854-1889 Misc papers inc staff [79]
1858-1884 Directors staff reports [16]
1859 John Melluish - memorial for post
[60]
1860's Appln form for clerk or salaried
officer [54]
1863 Security bond [55]
1871 W.Tucker, memorial re dismissal
[62]
1889 Amalg with GWR, staff details [40]

CORNWALL RAILWAY (Cont)
Public Record Office [Rail 630]
The following pieces are in respect of
Traffic dept staff and include similar
information for **South Devon Railway**
1873 Establishment Report [2]
1874 Establishment Report [3]

CORRIS RAILWAY
Corris Railway Society
Articles of a biographical nature are
published from time to time in the
Society's annual journal.

CROMFORD & HIGH PEAK RAILWAY
See L&NWR (PRO Rail 410/1309) page 35

DEVON AND SOMERSET RAILWAY
Incorp 1864. Amalg with GWR 1901.
Oxfordshire Record Office
1872 Parties to marriage settlement re
D&SR shares [WatX/1]

EAST AND WEST JUNCTION RAILWAY
Incorp 1864. To S-u-A & Mid 1908
Public Record Office
See Stratford-upon-Avon & Midland
Junction Railway [11] page 55

EAST LINCOLNSHIRE RAILWAY JOINT
   COMMITTEE
Incorp 1846. Leased to Great Northern
1848 and managed by Committee.
Public Record Office [Rail 177]
1848-1850 Pay lists, P.Way staff, police,
construction workers, etc [21]

EAST LONDON RAILWAY JOINT CTTEE
East London Railway auth 1882. Leased to
LB&SC, South Eastern, LC&D, Met.
and Met. District from 1884.
Public Record Office [Rail 179]
1884 Tffc staff (comp with 1890) [37]

EASTERN COUNTIES RAILWAY
Incorp 1836 as Grand Eastern Counties.
Amalg with others in Norfolk and
Suffolk to form Great Eastern 1862.
See **Unclassified items (Mr. Frank Cossey)**
page 57

Public Record Office [Rail 186]
1851-1857 Loco repairs, Stratford Works
with staff details [105]

EDEN VALLEY RAILWAY
Incorp 1858. Amalg with Stockton &
Darlington 1862.
Public Record Office [Rail 189]
1858 Paybill ledger [12]

EDINBURGH PERTH AND DUNDEE
   RAILWAY
Incorp 1845 as Edinburgh & Northern.
Name changed to EP&D 1849. Vested
in North British Rly 1862.
Scottish Record Office [BR/EPD/15]
1856 Staff book [1]

EXETER RAILWAY
Incorp 1883
Public Record Office [Rail 1057]
1883-1907 Stn Masters, house applns
[178]

FORTH BRIDGE RAILWAY
Incorp 1873. Worked/leased by North
British from 1882.
Scottish Record Office [BR/FOR/15]
Time and wages books

1912-1914 [1]	1914-1916 [2]
1916-1918 [3]	1918-1919 [4]
1919-1921 [5]	1921-1923 [6]
1923-1925 [7]	1925-1927 [8]
1927-1929 [9]	1929-1930 [10]
1931-1932 [11]	1932-1934 [12]
1934-1936 [13]	1936-1937 [14]
1937-1939 [15]	1939-1940 [16]
1940-1941 [17]	1941-1943 [18]
1943-1944 [19]	1944-1945 [20]
1945-1947 [21]	1947-1948 [22]

FURNESS RAILWAY
Incorp 1844.
Cumbria Record Office (Barrow)
Microfilm of PRO records reference *Rail
214 (97-103)*. Registers 102 and 103
include Barrow HQ staff and principal
employees at locations e.g. Barrow
harbour and Furness Abbey Hotel.

Public Record Office [Rail 214]
1852-1920 Staff register [102]
1867-1874 Reg, Traffic dept [97]
1868-1922 Staff register [103]
1874-1876 Reg, Traffic dept [98]
1876-1889 Reg, Traffic dept [99]
1889-1891 Reg, Traffic dept [100]
1891-1901 Reg, Traffic dept [101]

FURNESS RAILWAY (Cont)
Public Record Office [Rail 1057]
1844-1917 List of Directors with
biographical detail [3328]

GLASGOW AND SOUTH WESTERN RAILWAY
Incorp 1847
Scottish Record Office [BR/GSW/15]
1900-1902 Wages, loco works [2]
1902-1904 Wages, wagon works [3]
1902-1909 (with gaps) Barassie
workshops piecework rates etc [4-11]
1904-1905 Barassie workshops and else-
where, piecework [12]
1913-1920 Reg Barassie workshops [15]

Scottish Record Office
D L Smith Collection [GD422]
1874-1922 Register, uniform staff [1/89]

GREAT CENTRAL RAILWAY
In 1846 five companies amalgamated to
form Manchester, Sheffield &
Lincolnshire. In 1847 MS&L took over
two more. Name changed to Great
Central in 1897.
Public Record Office [Rail 226]
1857-1913 Staff book No.1 Secretary's
Office [193]
1913-1920 ditto No.2 [194]
1920-1923 ditto No.3 [195]

1867-1920 Reg of Officers, Asst.Officers
and Chief Clerks [234]
1872-1949 Reg, Goods dept Leicester
[199]
1882-on Officers' staff reg [196]
1893-1915 Labouring class houses at
Loughborough built by MS&L Rly
in 1896 [178] Plans [179]
1899-1946 Staff history book Goods dept
Leicester [198]
1900 Dismissal shop foremen, Gorton
[404]
1906-1920 Clerical staff age 60 and over
rec for retirement or retention [508]
c1915-1923 Sack depot Grimsby, staff
record book [197]
1920-1922 Pay and service of staff
employed on railway-owned canals
[192]

GREAT CENTRAL RAILWAY (Cont)
Public Record Office [Rail 226] (Cont)
Staff records
For records prior to 1899 **see Manchester,
Sheffield & Lincolnshire Railway,
pages 41 and 42.**
1899-1900 [200] Index [201]
1900-1902 [202] Index [203]
1903 [204] Index [205]
1903-1906 [206] Index [207]
1906-1907 [208] Index [209]
1907-1910 [210] Index [211]
1 Jan 1910 [226]
1910-1912 [212] Index [213]
1912-1913 [214] Index [215]
1913-1914 [216] Index [217]
1914-1918 [218] Index [219]
1918-1920 [220] Index [221]
1920-1923 [222] Index [223]
1923-1926 [224] Index [225]
1919-1927 Audit Accountant [227]

Registers of staff at Joint Agencies etc
For records prior to 1897 **see Manchester,
Sheffield & Lincolnshire Railway, page
42.**
1897-1906 [228] Index [229]
1906-1922 [230] Index [231]
1921-1925 [232] Index [233]

GREAT EASTERN RAILWAY
Incorp 1862 by amalgamation of Eastern
Counties and other railways in Norfolk
and Suffolk.
Public Record Office [Rail 227]
1853-1911 Reg Loco wagon shop No 1
[535]
1858-1903 Reg Goods dept, clerical and
wages, Bishopsgate [487]
1860-1918 Reg clerical staff [447]
1866-1933 Reg Temple Mills wagon
shops [533]
1870-1913 Staff contract reg, Audit dept
[448]
1870-1919 Reg Officers and clerks
salaries [449]
c1870-1922 Sack Supt's Office staff
record book [446]
1877-1930 Reg Carriage Workshop [540]
1888-1919 Sack dept staff lists [371]
1892-1894 Bishopsgate station,
misdemeanour and punishments book
[342]

GREAT EASTERN RAILWAY (Cont)
Public Record Office [Rail 227] (Cont)
1901-1936 Reg Temple Mills wagon
  shops **(Closed for 50 years)** [534]
1910 Retirement presentation, John
  Wilson Engineer in Chief [363]
1914 LC&W dept staff details [445]
1942-1946 Staff alterations, all depots:
  entering/leaving service; engine
  cleaners who have completed 250
  firing turns; transfers; staff joining and
  returning after miltary service
  (Closed for 50 years) [542]

Stratford Depot registers
* Closed for 50 years
1875-1958 Carr & Wagon engrs: A-W
  [543*]
1879-1940 Staff of depts of Accountant,
  Chief Mech Engr, Loco Running Supt,
  Chemist, Road Motor Engr, Electrical
  Power House [544*]
1886-1955 Chief Mech Engr: A-W [545*]
1899-1954   ditto   A-Z [546*]
1896-1955   ditto   K-R [547*]
1897-1955   ditto   D-J [548*]
1899-1953   ditto   A-C [549*]
1895-1955 Elec & Mech Engr: A-C
  [550*]
1902-1955   ditto   D-H [551*]
1913-1955   ditto   I-O [552*]
1911-1955   ditto   T-Y [553*]

Registers of salaried staff histories
Superintendent's dept
1855-1923 [450]   1864-1923 [452]
1857-1923 [453]   1873-1923 [454]
1862-1922 [451]   1914-1923 [455]
Goods
1868-1923 [456]   1871-1923 [457]
Passenger
1875-1917 [458]

Registers of wages staff histories
Traffic
1858-1924 [462]   1867-1924 [460]
1858-1924 [466]   1867-1924 [470]
1858-1925 [465]   1867-1925 [469]
1859-1924 [459]   1875-1922 [479]
1861-1923 [461]   1877-1930 [475]
1862-1925 [464]   1881-1920 [478]
1863-1927 [471]   1882-1928 [473]
1865-1924 [467]   1883-1929 [474]
1865-1930 [476]   1889-1930 [477]

GREAT EASTERN RAILWAY (Cont)
Public Record Office [Rail 227] (Cont)
Registers of wages staff histories
Traffic (Cont)
1866-1925 [463]   1893-1927 [472]
1866-1925 [468]
Goods
1872-1924 [485]   1877-1929 [484]
1873-1929 [483]   1892-1924 [480]
1876-1925 [482]   1894-1930 [486]
1877-1928 [481]
Drivers and firemen
1904-1911 [514]   1912-1921 [518]
1909-1918 [515]   1913-1919 [519]
1905-1919 [516]   1918-1919 [520]
1911-1919 [517]   Index [521]

Awards and cautions registers
* Closed for 50 years
1876-1950 Works staff: A-W [522*]
1897-1948   ditto   O-P [523*]
1900-1948   ditto   L-Z [524*]
1942-1950   ditto   S-W [525*]
1947-1950   ditto   A-J [526*]
1904-1920 Loco staff   I-N [527]
1913-1949   ditto   A-J [528*]
1915-1949   ditto   C [529*]
1936-1949   ditto   D-J [530*]
1937-1949   ditto   A-C [531*]
1940-1950   ditto   K-R [532*]

GREAT NORTH OF ENGLAND RAILWAY
Incorp 1836. Sold to Newcastle and
  Darlington Junction Rly 1846.
Public Record Office [Rail 232]
1840-1842 Paybill book [54]
1842-1847 Paybill book [55]

GREAT NORTH OF SCOTLAND RAILWAY
Incorp 1846
Aberdeen University Library
1853-1949 Reg guards and brakesmen
1865-1884 Pass dept staff changes
1865-1897 Pass dept job applications
1897-1903 Pass dept. Reg of staff off
  duty
1899-1925 (some gaps) Salary bills
1902-1913 Pass dept. Reg of staff off
  duty
1908-1913 Pass dept job applications
1912-1922 Misc records re staff
  conditions and wages

GREAT NORTH OF SCOTLAND RAILWAY (Cont)
Aberdeen University Library (Cont)
1913-1921 Pass dept. Staff off duty
1920-1923 Reg, Goods dept
1921-1926 Pass dept. Staff off duty
1922 Sec. Councils. Nomination papers

Scottish Record Office [BR/GNS/4]
1863/1870 Staff at stns and offices [17]

Scottish Record Office [BR/GNS/15]
Passenger Dept Offence books
1870-1906 [1]   1885-1899 [2]
1899-1905 [3]   1905-1915 [4]
1916-1921 [5]   1921-1929 [6]

Pass. Dept staff changes
1885-1896 [7]   1896-1902 [8]
1902-1911 [9]   1911-1914 [10]
1914-1919 [11]   1919-1923 [12]

Pass Dept Stn registers
1865-1873 [13]   1873-1878 [14]
1888-1895 [15]   1888-1900 [16]
1900-1905 [17]   1905-1910 [18]
1910-1914 [19]   1914-1920 [20]

Supt's Dept registers
1867-1887 [21]   1880-1888 [22]
1885-1927 [23]

1910-1922 Allowances, retired staff [25]
1912-1914 Paybill, Pass Supt's dept
Aberdeen [24]
1915-1918 Reg staff at stations [28]
1926-1935 Staff at stations [26]
- 1930 Reg Inverurie Works [27]

GREAT NORTHERN RAILWAY
Incorp 1846 by amalgamation of Direct
Northern Rly and London & York Rly.
Public Record Office [Rail 236]
Sack Dept
c1861-1924 Staff register * [727]
1910-1925 Sickness book [728]
*From 1.1.1923 relates to **LNER**.

Locomotive Dept
1862-1913 Office staff reg. Indexed *
[730]
1862-1943 Salaried staff reg. Indexed
[729]

GREAT NORTHERN RAILWAY (Cont)
Public Record Office [Rail 236] (Cont)
1903-1916 Circulars re hours and pay of
Drivers & Firemen [731]
1915 Nov.18. Unfair promotion at
Bradford. Judge Parry's decision [732]

Regs of Drivers & Firemen with staff
histories
1848-1919 Leeds District [733]
1882-1919 Leeds District [734]
1883-1924 Leeds District [736]
1894-1924 Leeds District [735]
1894-1924 Index to 735 [737]

1848-1924 Seniority books, drivers and
firemen, Leeds, Ardsley, Bradford,
Ingrow and Holmfield [738 + 739]
1879-1919 Reg cleaners and firemen
recommended for promotion [740]
1889-1926 Reg, new entrants to Loco
dept, Leeds District * [741]
* From 1.1.1923 relates to **LNER**.

Superintendent's Office
1865-1872 Reg of clerks [743]
1865-1902 Reg of clerks [742]
1870-1912 Reg of clerks [744]
1886-1920 Reg, Supt's office clerks,
commencing dates including Army
Reserve list [745]

See **Unclassified items (Mr. Frank Cossey)**
page 57.

**GW AND MIDLAND RLY CO'S JOINT
COMMITTEE (CLIFTON EXTENSION)**
Auth 1867 as Bristol Port & Pier.
Transferred to GW&Midland Joint
1871.
Public Record Office [Rail 241]
1865-1915 Reg of staff [28]

GREAT WESTERN RAILWAY
Incorp 1835
Birmingham & Midland S.G.H.
1899-1907 Reg Tyseley Goods depot

Cheshire Record Office [NPR2/]
1870's-1950's Originally **Cambrian** latterly
GW. Central Wales Dist. Tffc dept
staff [26]
1880's-1950's Chester Div Tffc dept staff
reg. Indexed. [23]

GREAT WESTERN RAILWAY (Cont)
Cheshire Record Office (NPR2/) (Cont)

c1890-1945 Tffc dept staff reg. Mainly **Cambrian** but includes **GW** Central Wales Dist [27]

c1900-1950's Staff reg. Central Wales Dist. Mostly Goods but early years inc Tffc staff. Also includes some **Cambrian** [22]

1940's Staff circulars from Padd HQ to Div.Supt. Chester, also minutes of Staff Cttee 1942-1945, plus index 1939-1945 [24]

Cheshire Record Office

1924-25 Descriptive account of the Chester Division by J.Morris, Div. Supt. [D5034/1] *This comprehensive official report contains information on each station and depot in the Division. Staff establishments at each location, including the Supt's Office, are given by grade, but no names.*

Devon Record Office

1873-1874 George Stuart, policeman, service certificate [588M/F5]

c1917 W.P. Parkhouse, Inspector, Exeter, illuminated address on retirement [3644Z/Z1]

Oxfordshire Record Office

The following items contain references to railway employees:-

1881 H.W.Goffe, Birmingham [Lodd I/i/17]

1894 J.H.Ryman, Wolverhampton [Far.xxxv/iv/1]

1907 J.H.Ryman, Wolverhampton [Far.xxxv/iii/26]

1921 Francis William Showers, Padd [Var.xxvii/i/20 + 21,27]

1935 Joseph Pratley, Charlbury [Misc.Watney II/ii/58]

1947 Albert Welsh, 16 Tower Hill, Witney [Welch XLII/10]

Public Record Office [Rail 250]

1839-1840 Bristol sub-cttee app'ts [112]

Clerks appointments committee
1888-1903 [148]   1903-1923 [149]
1923-1934 [150]   1934-1939 [151]

GREAT WESTERN RAILWAY (Cont)
Public Record Office [Rail 250] (Cont)

Retiring allowances committee
1893-1905 [128]   1906-1917 [129]
1918-1924 [130]   1919-1934 [132]
1924-1928 [131]   1934-1939 [133]
1939-1947 [134]

Public Record Office [Rail 252]

1876-1888 Volume of Awards Nos.1-50 [17]

Public Record Office [Rail 253]

1840-1947 Directors and Officers histories and portraits [487]

1856-1877 Paybills, Chirk station [83]

1867 Loco staff: working arrangements, pay, conditions of service etc.[483]

1867-1871 Memoranda book of WILLIAM PRUSLOW (? Registrar, W'hpton) Includes staff movements etc [661]

1868-1884 Paybills, Gen Mgr's office [174+175]

1884 Duty book Stanton stn [445]

1889-1903 Loco staff: working arrangements, pay, conditions of service etc. [484]

1891-1928 Reading stn staff duties etc. Includes names and addresses of some of the staff [511+512]

1892 Standard cottages for station masters, signalmen, platelayers etc. Scale plans and designs [509]

c1904 Tickets for funerals of Queen Victoria and King George V to Mr.Bolland, GWR cricket team member [459]

1904-1910 L,C and Stores depts, Swindon job applications and correspondence [321]

1906 Testimonial volume to William Catton Station Master St.Columb Road [508]

1911-1945 Staff circulars, rates of pay, conditions of service etc. [485]

1919, 1921 Strike volunteers: arrangements [732]

1932-1934 CME's Dept, Swindon, job applns also staff accidents [322]

1934 Authorised staff establishment in Traffic dept at all stations [515]

GREAT WESTERN RAILWAY (Cont)
Public Record Office [Rail 257]
1849 Oct 22 Abstract of men employed at
Swindon [6]
1869-1888 Returns and lists of staff
employed in General Manager's and all
depts [8]
1879-1887 Enginemen. Pay, hours etc. [7]

Public Record Office [Rail 258]
1859-1947 Retention of gold passes by
retired directors and officers of other
companies and GWR [592]
1863-1930 Applns for issue/return of
permanent passes: letter book with
name index [598]
1870-1947 Regs of gold and other passes
issued to Directors and Officers of
GWR and other Companies [600-607]
1868-1905 Departmental staff returns
and charts [280]
c.1870-1947 Passes issued by various
railways, lists etc.[593]
1875-1912 Policy on retirement of staff,
with lists [412]
1875-1947 Gratuities (a) on retirement,
(b) retiring allowances,(c) to widows,
and (d) for special services rendered
[195]
1876-1920 Female clerical staff,
employment of [405]
1877-1914 Clerical staff: recruiting and
examination of [400]
1890-1931 Signal dept: organisation and
appointments [406]
1900-1946 Retired officers and
consultants [484]
1903 Sir Joseph L. Wilkinson, Gen Mgr,
death [283]
1904-1922 Salaried staff: increase in
salaries etc [404]
1908-1934 Directors; deaths of [291]
1911 Sir James C. Inglis, Gen Mgr,death
[284]
1919 Frank Potter, Gen. Mgr. death [285]
1921-1929 Salaried staff special training
scheme [403]
1921-1934 Special supplemental retiring
allowances [189]
1922 Charles Aldington, Gen Mgr, death
[286]
1927-1947 Special supplemental retiring
allowances [188]
1929 J.C.Lloyd, Ch. Engr, death [287]

GREAT WESTERN RAILWAY (Cont)
Public Record Office [Rail 258] (Cont)
1932-1944 Special supplemental retiring
allowances [191]
1933-1960 Correspondence re return of
gold passes [594]
1934 Viscount Churchill, death; Sir Robert
Horne, appt (both Chairmen) [281]
1935-1943 Special supplemental retiring
allowances [190]
1940 Viscount Horne, Chairman, death
[282]
1940-1947 Salaried staff retirements:
extracts from minutes etc [419]
1944-1945 The Directorate: historical
notes and functions [433]
1946-1947 Membership of Directors'
committees [432]

Public Record Office [Rail 264]
+ **Registers of drivers and firemen,
showing date entered service, fines,
promotions etc. With 3 index
volumes.**
Dates are approximate.

+ 1841-1864 [18]	+ 1864-1873 [20]
+ 1865-1867 [19]	+ 1866-1873 [22]
+ 1867-1869 [21]	+ 1873-1875 [23]
+ 1873-1915 [96]	+ 1875-1876 [25]
+ 1875-1877 [24]	+ 1875-1877 [26]
+ 1875-1878 [27]	+ 1880-1911 [94]
+ 1881-1882 [28]	+ 1881-1915 [95]
+ 1883-1884 [29]	+ 1884-1885 [30]
+ 1884-1903 [59]	+ 1885-1904 [58]
+ 1886-1887 [31]	+ 1886-1887 [32]
+ 1886-1888 [33]	+ 1888-1889 [35]
+ 1888-1911 [92]	+ 1889-1890 [34]
+ 1889-1892 [36]	+ 1889-1893 [37]
+ 1889-1920 [98]	+ 1890-1914 [93]
+ 1893-1894 [38]	+ 1893-1894 [39]
+ 1894-1895 [41]	+ 1895-1896 [40]
+ 1896-1897 [42]	+ 1897 [43]
+ 1897 [44]	+ 1897-1898 [45]
+ 1897-1899 [47]	+ 1897-1899 [49]
+ 1897-1914 [99]	+ 1898 [46]
+ 1898-1920 [104]	+ 1899 [50]
+ 1899-1900 [48]	+ 1899-1900 [51]
+ 1900 [52]	+ 1900-1913 [97]
+ 1901-1902 [54]	+ 1902 [55]
+ 1902-1903 [56]	+ 1903-1904 [57]
+ 1904 [62]	+ 1904-1905 [60]
+ 1905-1908 [63]	+ 1906-1907 [61]
+ 1908 [64]	+ 1909 [65]
+ 1909-1910 [66]	+ 1909-1913 [71]

GREAT WESTERN RAILWAY (Cont)
Public Record Office [Rail 264] (Cont)

+ 1910-1911 [67]   + 1910-1923 [103]
+ 1911 [70]   + 1911-1912 [68]
+ 1912 [69]   + 1912-1913 [73]
+ 1913-1914 [72]   + 1913-1914 [74]
+ 1913-1919 [82]   + 1914 [75]
+ 1914-1915 [76]   + 1914-1917 [81]
+ 1914-1917 [83]   + 1914-1918 [100]
+ 1915-1916 [77]   + 1915-1916 [78]
+ 1915-1916 [79]   + 1915-1917 [80]
+ 1915-1920 [106]   + 1918-1919 [84]
+ 1918-1920 [91]   + 1919 [85]
+ 1919 [86]   + 1919 [87]
+ 1919-1920 [88]   + 1919-1920 [105]
+ 1920 [89]   + 1920 [90]
+ 1920-1923 [107]   + 1923-1924 [108]
+ 1923-1925 [109]   + 1923-1934 [112]
+ 1925-1934[111]   + 1927-1930 [110]
+ 1932-1936 [114]   + 1933-1936 [115]
+ 1934-1935 [113]   + 1935-1937 [118]
+ 1935-1939 [121]   + 1936 [116]
+ 1936-1937 [117]   + 1936-1937 [119]
+ 1936-1938 [120]   + 1936-1940 [122]
+ 1937-1940 [126]   + 1938-1940 [123]
+ 1938-1940 [124]   + 1938-1941 [127]
+ 1938-1941 [129]   + 1939-1941 [125]
+ 1939-1941 [130]   + 1941 [128]
+ Index 1 from 1 March 1906 [131]
+ Index 2 from 17 Feb 1920 [132]
+ Index [133]

* **Record books of Loco & Carr dept staff at stations and depots by Division, showing name, grade and rate of pay**
Old Oak Common Division
* 1840-1874 [135]   * 1875-1884 [137]
* 1870-1895 [141]   * 1875-1888 [138]
* 1870-1897 [140]   * 1879-1909 [144]
* 1872-1879 [136]   * 1887-1915 [145]
* 1872-1914 [147]   * 1903-1915 [146]

Swindon Division
* 1863-1911 [152]   * 1884-1911 [151]
* 1866-1919 [158]   * 1884-1916 [155]
* 1870-1872 [148]   * 1884-1920 [159]
* 1872-1915 [154]   * 1887-1912 [153]
* 1874-1896 [149]   * 1888-1920 [160]
* 1882-1920 [161]   * 1896-1914 [157]
* 1883-1916 [156]   * 1898-1908 [150]

GREAT WESTERN RAILWAY (Cont)
Public Record Office [Rail 264] (Cont)
Bristol Division
* 1846-1903 [165]   * 1865-1914 [168]
* 1860-1883 [166]   * 1870-1916 [171]
* 1861-1903 [164]   * 1874-1920 [173]
* 1862-1914 [169]   * 1876-1880 [162]
* 1864-1898 [167]   * 1877-1884 [163]

Newton Abbot Division
* 1846-1880 [174]   * 1860-1913 [180]
* 1846-1884 [175]   * 1870-1919 [185]
* 1850-1916 [184]   * 1872-1910 [181]
* 1857-1897 [177]   * 1875-1916 [182]
* 1859-1890 [176]   * 1876-1916 [183]
* 1859-1910 [178]   * 1880-1920 [186]
* 1859-1910 [179]   * 1889-1920 [187]

Newport Division
* 1840-1907 [190]   * 1880-1920 [199]
* 1851-1902 [192]   * 1880-1920 [201]
* 1865-1915 [197]   * 1880-1921 [198]
* 1866-1897 [189]   * 1882-1902 [193]
* 1871-1915 [196]   * 1890-1920 [202]
* 1876-1884 [188]   * 1891-1907 [191]
* 1876-1915 [195]   * 1898-1915 [194]
* 1878-1920 [200]

Neath Division
* 1843-1913 [212]   * 1864-1900 [207]
* 1851-1876 [203]   * 1867-1913 [214]
* 1852-1904 [210]   * 1871-1907 [213]
* 1855-1883 [206]   * 1872-1888 [204]
* 1855-1902 [209]   * 1873-1915 [215]
* 1856-1880 [205]   * 1873-1916 [216]
* 1857-1907 [211]   * 1884-1920 [218]
* 1859-1901 [208]

Wolverhampton Division
* 1856-1898 [222]   * 1870-1915 [224]
* 1864-1905 [221]   * 1873-1913 [225]
* 1866-1913 [226]   * 1877-1920 [231]
* 1867-1906 [219]   * 1891-1920 [234]
* 1867-1920 [230]   * 1894-1921 [232]
* 1868-1916 [229]   * 1895-1907 [223]
* N.D. [233]

Worcester Division
* 1859-1902 [236]   * 1875-1907 [235]
* 1860-1916 [238]   * 1876-1920 [239]
* 1862-1913 [237]   * 1884-1921 [240]

GREAT WESTERN RAILWAY (Cont)
Public Record Office [Rail 264] (Cont)
The following are memorandum books re
  Loco staff matters, including medical
  exams and eyesight tests
1900-1932 [10]   Index [17]
1903-1908 [11]   Index [17]
1908-1912 [12]   Index [17]
1911-1921 [13]   Index [17]
1921-1935 [14]   Index [17]
1929-1937 [15]   Index [17]
1938-1946 [16]   Index [17]

The following three series are registers of
  uniformed staff

Series 1

1838-1915 [345]	1842-1915 [353]
1839-1915 [346]	1843-1915 [351]
1839-1915 [349]	1845-1915 [348]
1841-1915 [347]	1845-1915 [350]
1842-1915 [342]	1846-1915 [352]
1842-1915 [343]	1848-1915 [341]

Index to series 1 [458]

Series 2

1864-1915 [362]	1873-1915 [366]
1870-1915 [357]	1877-1915 [359]
1870-1915 [360]	1878-1915 [356]
1872-1915 [358]	1890-1915 [355]
1873-1915 [361]	1891-1915 [364]
1873-1915 [363]	1895-1915 [354]
1873-1915 [365]	

Index to series 2 [459]

Series 3

1868-1915 [373]	1883-1915 [377]
1878-1915 [375]	1887-1915 [372]
1889-1915 [368]	1880-1915 [378]
1894-1915 [369]	1881-1915 [379]
1897-1915 [371]	1882-1915 [374]
1898-1915 [370]	N.D. [376]

Index to series 3 [460]

The following * are registers of weekly
  staff, passenger and goods
* 1893-1913 Birmingham Division [416]
* 1896-1906 London Division [415]
* 1898-1906 Bristol Division [421]
* 1898-1907 Exeter Division [422]
* 1898-1907 Hereford Division [418]
* 1898-1907 Worcester Division [419]
* 1898-1909 Chester Division [417]
* 1898-1914 Cardiff Division [420]

GREAT WESTERN RAILWAY (Cont)
Public Record Office [Rail 264] (Cont)
* 1898-1915 Bristol, Exeter & Plymouth
  Divisions [423]
* 1905-1912 Cardiff Division [425]
* 1907-1915 Pontypool Road Divn [426]
* 1910-1915 Birmingham Division [427]
* 1910-1915 Chester Division [424]

+ **Registers of traffic staff at stations in
  Wales**

+1861-1919 [430]	+1882-1935 [439]
+1871-1903 [431]	+1898-1934 [433]
+1872-1892 [438]	+1904-1919 [432]
+1872-1923 [436]	+1908-1923 [435]
+1873-1923 [437]	+1909-1923 [434]

1910-1914 Alphabetical register of
  characters * [264]
1915-1918 ditto * [265]
1918-1927 ditto * [266]
* These seem to be index volumes to a
  series which has not survived
1946-1947 Reg of enquiries re character
  from prospective employers, with
  index to names of employees [267]

1835-1910 Reg of clerks entered service
  [1-9]
1835-1860 Reg clerks + index
  [401+402]
1835-1863 Reg clerks + index
  [394+395]
1836-1867 Reg clerks + index
  [397+398]
1838-1848 Reg clerks [403]
1838-1853 Reg clerks [404]
1838-1863 Reg clerks [379]
1838-1876 Reg clerks + index
  [399+400]
1838-1902 Reg LC&WD wkly paid staff
  [246]
1839-1877 Reg inspectors, booking
  porters, booking constables [414]
1840-1874 Reg LCD OOC Div [135]
1840-1944 Reg LC&WD officers,
  draughtsmen, clerks and lad clerks
  [254] (For continuation see 245,
  1880-1941)
1841-1904 Reg audit clerks [441]
1843-1940 Reg Accts dept clerks
  [409+410]

GREAT WESTERN RAILWAY (Cont)
Public Record Office [Rail 264] (Cont)
1845-1902 Reg LC&WD staff
  [276 + 277]
1846-1944 Reg LC&WD wkly paid
  foremen, inspectors etc [258]
1848-1902 Reg LC&WD clerks,
  draughtsmen, Supts [275]
1850-1887 Reg LC&WD officers,
  draughtsmen, inspectors, foremen
  etc [269 + 270]
1850-1924 Reg PWay dep, W'hpton area,
  inspectors, sub-insprs, foremen
  entered service 1850-1909 [449]
c1851-1901 Reg Stationery & ticket
  printing dep [444]
1852-1954 Reg LC&WD weekly paid
  clerks and messengers [256 + 257]
1853-1855 Reg clerks [405]
1854-1899 Bristol Div.Tffc staff reg.
  Surnames A and B [470]
1858-1899 Reg LC&WD clerks
  [272 + 273]
1859-1908 Reg LC&WD clerks [278]
1860-1926 Reg Eng offices, Whpton
  [450]
1863-1865 Reg clerks [396]
1867-1923 Reg LC&WD enginemen
  amalgamated lines [310]
1869-1881 Paybills LC&WD [296-299]
1870-1911 Reg lad clerks [384-393]
c1870-1922 Reg unidentified (includes
  some Cardiff DSO histories) [457]
1872-1913 Reg Loco Accounts [271]
1873-1923 Reg LC&WD **late Brecc ι &
  Merthyr, Neath & Brecon, Alexaιdra
  (Newport & S.Wales) Dock and Rly**
  [301]
1874-1923 Reg LC&WD Oswestry [303]
1874-1925 Reg LC&WD officers, sal
  staff and supervisors **from amalg lines**
  [307]
1876-1877 Paybills Reading station [429]
1879-1934 Timebooks LC&WD pupils
  [287-291]
1880-1941 Reg LC&WD salaried staff
  [245]   (Seems to be continuation of
  254, 1840-1944)
1880-1962 Reg audit clerks, inc females
  and clerks **from amalg lines** [442]
1880-1962 Reg Ch. Acct's audit section
  clerks [443]
1881-1938 Reg LC&WD Swindon stn
  staff [242]   Index [244]

GREAT WESTERN RAILWAY (Cont)
Public Record Office [Rail 264] (Cont)
1883-1938 Reg LC&WD Swindon stn
  staff [241]   Index [244]
1882-1938 Reg LC&WD O.O.Common,
  Bristol, N.Abbot Divisions [243]
  Index [244]
1883-1911 Advances, vacs, LC&WD
  clerks [323-327]
1883-1927 Reg LC&WD sal staff **from
  amalg lines** (Docks & Elec deps) [308]
1884-1923 Reg LC&WD **late Cardiff Bute
  Dock, Cardiff Gas Works, Llanelly &
  Mynydd-Mawr Railways** [302]
1886-1923 Reg LC&WD **late Taff Vale
  Railway** [305 + 306]
1887-1910 Reg LC&WD office boys and
  messengers [268] (For continuation
  see 255, 1910-1923)
1888-1913 Reg LC&WD stn staff
  [248 + 249]
1889-1923 Reg **late Rhymney Rly** [304]
1890-1901 Reg LC&WD weekly paid
  shop clerks, time and store keepers
  [250]
1891-1914 Reg PWay staff pensions
  Wolverhampton Dist [451]
1892-1923 Reg LC&WD **(ex Barry Rly)**
  [300]
1892-1925 Stn regs LC&WD weekly paid
  staff, shop clerks, time and store
  keepers [251 - 253]
1894-1908 Reg staff changes,
  promotions, Aylesbury Joint station
  GW & Met [411]
1899-1909 Reg clerks perm. apptd [406]
1900-1907 Record book LC&WD
  candidates for shunting firemen [320]
1900-1958 Reg loco dept clerks and
  foremen in Wales [some ex wages
  staff] [440]
1902 Sig dept staff Reading Works [428]
1903-1924 Reg Elec Engr's dept
  [333 + 334]
1905-1913 Reg weekly staff London
  District [382]
1910-1923 Reg LC&WD office boys and
  messengers [255] (Appears to be
  continuation of 268, 1887-1910)
1910-1940 Reg LC&WD female clerks
  [261 + 262]
1911-1919 Reg new clerks [408]
1912-1916 Reg clerks promoted [407]

GREAT WESTERN RAILWAY (Cont)
Public Record Office [Rail 264] (Cont)
1913-1925 Station reg LC&WD salaried staff, foremen, inspectors and draughtsmen [247]

1914-1919 Pension book LC&WD [332]

1914-1921 Reg LC&WD clerks etc [321]

1914-1935 Reg LC&WD cleaners [263]

1915-1929 LC&WD charts of supervisory and technical staff [315+316]

1915-1929 LC&WD charts of clerical staff [317+318]

1918 Elec Engr's dept staff census [335]

1918-1938 Reg newly appointed uniformed staff [380+381]

1919-1930 Stn reg LC&WD salaried staff, officers, technical, male and female clerks [259+260]

1920-1921 Bristol Div reports on station staff [453]

1920-1952 Reg Permanent way staff pensions, Wolverhampton District, includes medical exams and eyesight tests [452]

1922 First and special class officers and staff **employed by constituent companies in Western Group** [337]

1922 LC&WD supervisors and clerks taken over from **Barry, Cambrian, Alexandra (Newport & S.Wales) Dock and Rly** [311to 313]

1922 Staff alterations, salaried and supervisory staff [338]

1922 Traffic dept staff establishment at stations and offices [340]

c1923 LC&WD drivers, firemen and cleaners **from amalgamated railways** [309+310]

1923-1927 LC&WD vacancies, technical, supervisory and technical [328 - 331]

1923-1935 Staff discharged through trade depression promised reinstatement; juniors (19½ years and over) in service to be provided for in adult posts; applns for transfer; redundant staff in initial grades [469]

1925 Auth staff establishment [339]

1928 Elec Engr's dept staff census [336]

1932-1934 Reg LC&WD new workshops staff [274]

1932-1937 Charts LC&WD supervisory and clerical staff Dock Mech Engr's offices [314]

GREAT WESTERN RAILWAY (Cont)
Public Record Office [Rail 264] (Cont)
1939-1951 Reg Oswestry Works staff [412]

1956-1962 Reg Oswestry Works staff [413]

N.D. Index to register of salaried staff appointed and dismissed. Register wanting. [463]

Statements of salaried clerical positions

N.D. Traffic dept [465]

N.D. Goods dept [466]

N.D. Stn masters, goods agents, yard masters [467]

N.D. Secretary's, Accountant's, Loco, Engineering, Stores, Signal, Surveyor's, Electrical, Stationery, and Marine Depts. Plymouth Docks, Special Police and Widows and Orphans Fund [468]

Public Record Office [Rail 1014]
N.D. Lists of Directors and Officers [27/1-17]

1842 Memorial from Michael Driscoll (a suspended servant of the Coy) in the hope that he will be reinstated "and to obliterate any stigma that may attach to his character" [4/5]

1841-1843 Appln for appt as Porter etc [3/34]

1842-1890 Papers relating to James Hurst, the GWR first engine driver [8/3]

1847 General regulations of the GWR for the employment of Superintendents, Accountants, Storekeepers, Booking Clerks etc [4/40]

1863-1866 Staff employed in the Secretary's Office [6/39]

1908 Letter from Irish youth asking for an appointment [8/16/2]

Public Record Office [Rail 1057]
1889-1917 Sig Telegraph and Elect Engr's dept: resignation of Mr. Spagnoletti 1892; appt of Mr.Goodenough 1892-1903, list of staff 1896-1903 [2933]

GREAT WESTERN RAILWAY
MECHANICS INSTITUTE,SWINDON
Public Record Office [Rail 276]
1848-1947 Notices, photos etc, and
reports of Swindon & North Wilts
Tech School 1892-1906 [22]

HAMPSTEAD JUNCTION RAILWAY
Incorp 1853. Transferred to L&NW 1863.
Public Record Office [Rail 291]
1857-1859 Check time book [6]
1857-1860 Pay book [7]

HIGHLAND RAILWAY
Incorp 1865
Scottish Record Office [BR/HR/15]
1878-1920 Reg of clerkship applicants [1]
c1912-1917 Staff reg [7]
c1918-1920 Staff reg [8]
1919-1923 Reg of clerkship applicants [2]
1921-1923 Reg of clerical candidates [3]
1921-c1927 Staff reg [9]

HULL AND BARNSLEY RAILWAY
Incorp 1880. Became part of North
Eastern Rly 1922.
Public Record Office [Rail 312]
1885-1922 Tffc dept uniform staff [77]
1885-1927 Drivers and firemen [80 + 81]
1890-1925 Goods & docks dept staff [78]
1913-1921 Wages statements and staff
statistics [79]

Tyne and Wear Archive Service
1900-1922 Super fund contributions book
[992/4]

HULL AND HOLDERNESS RAILWAY
Incorp 1853. Worked by North Eastern Rly
from 1860 and vested in NER 1862.
Public Record Office [Rail 313]
1859 Fortnightly wages pay lists [22]

HULL AND SELBY RAILWAY
Incorp 1836. Leased to York & North
Midland from 1845. Sold to NER
1872.
Public Record Office [Rail 315]
1845-1875 Staff reg [30]

ISLE OF WIGHT RAILWAY
Originally Isle of Wight Eastern section
1860, name changed to Isle of Wight
1863.
Public Record Office [Rail 328/
1864-1915 Staff register [16]
1884-1923   "   "   [17]
These two items are filed with Isle of
Wight Central Railway

ISLE OF WIGHT CENTRAL RAILWAY
Incorp 1887
Public Record Office [Rail 328]
1860-1915 Staff register, includes record
of watches and clocks, 1933-1962
[18]
1907-1912 Misc records including
apprentices indenture of agreement
etc. [14]

LANCASHIRE & YORKSHIRE & GREAT
NORTHERN JOINT STATIONS
COMMITTEE
Incorp 1851
Public Record Office [Rail 341]
1894-1913 Minutes of Joint Stations
Committee [6]
(Contains list of staff changes and
advances)

LANCASHIRE AND YORKSHIRE RAILWAY
Various companies amalgamated in 1836
to form the Manchester & Leeds.
Name changed to Lancashire and
Yorkshire 1847.
*Greater Manchester County Record Office
[A18]*
The following records are for HORWICH
WORKS
Late 19thC-early 20thC Staff history
cards. In six groups by surname
(A-C, C-G, G-J, J-P, P-S, S-Z) and
Outdoor Machinery staff [5/1-7]
1908 Workmens register [7/1]
1937,1946 Piecework rates [7/2]
1938-1980 Employees collection fund
[6/1-8]

Public Record Office [Rail 343]
1851 Officer's notebook with list of
Officers for 1850 [722]
1853-1872 Time book, Hindley stn [845]
1863-1941 Reg Bacup loco dept **(includes
LNWR and LMSR)** [844]

LANCASHIRE & YORKSHIRE RAILWAY (Cont)

Public Record Office [Rail 343] (Cont)

1865-1879 General Orders from Traffic Mgr's Office. Includes Inspectors reports 1866-79. [764]

1887-1927 Reg loco drivers and firemen **(includes LNWR and LMSR)** [843]

1903-1905 Pay lists Chief Traffic Manager [835]

1903-1905 Pay lists Secretary [838]

1903-1907 Pay lists Acct's dept [827]

1903-1917 Special arrangements book, with list of clothing supplied to staff [723]

1908-1912 Pay lists Acct's dept [828]

1908-1913 Officers' salaries, Chief Cashier's dept [829]

1910-1911 Pay lists Chief Traffic Manager [836]

1913-1915 Pay lists Chief Cashier's dept [831]

1913-1921 Officers' salaries, Chief Cashier's dept [830]

1915-1918 Pay lists Chief Cashier's dept [832]

1915-1921 Salary advances of Officials and Supervisory staff, Traffic etc depts [842]

1917-1921 Pay lists personal staff Chief Goods Manager [834]

1918-1919 Pay lists Chief Cashier's dept [833]

1919-1921 Pay lists Supt of Line [839]

1921-1922 Pay lists Supt of Line [840] *

1922-1923 Pay lists Gen Supt [841] *

1922-1924 Pay lists Div Acct [837] *

* (From 1 Jan 1922 relates to **L&NW** and from 1 Jan 1923 to **LM&S Rly**)

Public Record Office [Rail 623]

1862-1897 Joint station records **included in Shropshire Union** [67 + 68]

LANCASHIRE, DERBYSHIRE & EAST COAST RAILWAY

Incorp 1891. Sold to Great Central 1907

Public Record Office [Rail 344]

1904-1906 Appt of Mr. Harry Willmott as General Manager and Chief Officer, various agreements concerning [56]

LANCASTER AND CARLISLE RAILWAY

Incorp 1844. Worked by L&NW 1859, vested in L&NW 1879

See L&NW Rly [1862] page 37

LEEDS NORTHERN RAILWAY

Originally Leeds & Thirsk 1845. Name changed to Leeds Northern 1851. To NE Rly 1854.

Public Record Office [Rail 357]

1845-1846 Bramhope contract time book [36]

1846 Pannal contract time book [37]

1846-1849 General time book [38]

1847-1858 Wages book Bramhope contract Inspector's dept and Goods dept Wellington Street [29]

1850-1853 List of staff and incomes [33]

LIVERPOOL AND MANCHESTER RAILWAY

Incorp 1826. Consolidated with others in 1845 to form the Grand Junction Rly. Latter with London & Birmingham and Manchester & Birmingham formed London & North Western 1846.

Public Record Office [Rail 371]

1839-1845 Salary lists 1845 with earlier salary receipts [23]

1841 May-1845 June Monthly bonuses paid to clerks of L & M Rly by Grand Junction Rly (incomplete) [32]

LLANELLY RAILWAY AND DOCK COMPANY

Incorp 1835. Worked by GWR from 1873. Absorbed by GWR 1889.

Public Record Office [Rail 377]

1873 Staff lists [30]

1889 Reports etc re amalgamation with GWR [32]

LONDON AND BIRMINGHAM RAILWAY

Incorp 1833. Consolidated with Grand Junction and Manchester & Birmingham to form L&NW 1846.

Oxfordshire Record Office

The following contains references to a railway employee:-

c1830's John Jelly [CH.CV 1]

LONDON AND BIRMINGHAM RLY Cont)

Public Record Office [Rail 384]
1833-1838 Establishment papers [258]
1833-1846 Salaries reg [284]
1834 Establishment London office [291]
1834-1835 Contractors wage & petty cash book [254]
1835-1836 Abstracts of men employed in London and Birmingham Divns [204 + 205]
1837 Further railway opening. Moorsom's report on staff [126]
1838 Sept. Letter from E.Bury (contractor) to Moorsom (Secy) re houses at Wolverton, built for accommodation of enginemen, being already occupied [280/24]
1838 Oct Formation of Audit dept. Report by Kenneth Morrison [129]
1838-1847 Regs of permanent officers and servants (indexed) [285 - 289]

Public Record Office [Rail 386]
1845 Agt with Peter Clarke accepting position of General Supt [71]

LONDON & NORTH EASTERN RAILWAY

Aberdeen University Library
These items are in respect of the Northern Scottish Area.
1882-1943 Salaried staff date of birth book. Gives designation, station, date joined service and remarks. Seems to have been kept 1947-57
1924-1930 Traffic dept. Reg of staff changes
1925 Advances of salary, managing, clerical and supervisory staff for month ending 31st May
1938 Traffic dept. Staff book
1938-1944 Reg of staff changes. This book is fragile, not able to stand much handling or photocopying.

This item is in respect of the Southern Scottish Area.
1925 Advances of salary, managing, clerical and supervisory staff for month ending 31st May

LONDON & NORTH EASTERN RAILWAY (Cont)

Doncaster Central Library
Material is available, accessible only through Local History Section indexes

Northamptonshire Record Office
1935 Woodford Perway District gang cards [ZA 230]
c1940 Woodford Halse Reg [ZA 361]

Public Record Office [Rail 393]
1897-1927 Stn Master's staff books, Gainsborough Lincs [225 + 226]

Public Record Office [Rail 397]
c1920-1938 Reg staff appointments and salaries, Bow & Old Ford stn [11]
1929 Loco dept Officers salaries [6]
1939 Staff at stns & depots [1-3]
Various. Drivers, firemen and motormen timebook Heaton steam shed 1923 and South Gosforth electric shed 1923-1929 [8]

Scottish Record Office [BR/LNE/15]
1922-1940 S.C.No3 minutes [54]
1923-1935 S.C.No5 minutes [56]
1923-1939 S.C.No2 memos [53]
1925 Staff lists [69]
c1925-1935 Staff books, salaried staff Central & Southern. Fife & Northern and Western sections [38-40]
1925-1937 Staff accidents reports and corres, discipline offences [57-68]
1925-1964 S.C.No2 sub-committee reports [52]
1926-1939 S.C.No4 minutes [55]
1928-1943 Reg temp staff at depots [70]
1930-1943 Offence book [4]
1931-1935 Att books Div Accountant, Edinburgh [85 + 86]
1931-1939 Staff summaries, Loco dep, Scottish Area [71]
1933-1935 Applicants for clerkships [42]
1934-1945 Wages staff books, Scottish Area [72 + 73] Indexes [74-77]
1935-1944 Job applications [41]
1937-1947 Candidates for junior clerks entrance exams [43]

LONDON & NORTH EASTERN RLY (Cont)
Scottish Record Office (BR/LNE/15) (Cont)
1942-1946 S.C.No.1 sub-committee
reports [51]
1945-1947 Operating staff book [80]
1946-1950 Operating staff book Abbey
Hill- Pomathorn [81]
1946-1950 Operating staff book
Portobello-Woodburn [82]
1946-1954 Staff book Passenger and
Goods Managers' [83]

Scottish Record Office
A G Dunbar Collection [GD344]
1871-1930 Staff book Kipps shed **inc NB**
[2/36]
1880-1932 Staff book Parkhead and
Burnbank sheds, **inc NB** [2/37]
1922-1935 Staff seniority list Polmont
shed, **inc NB** [2/35]
1932-1939 Staff book Parkhead shed
[8/3]

LONDON AND NORTH WESTERN
RAILWAY
Incorp 1846 by numerous amalgamations
Bedfordshire Record Office
1921-1923 Potton station. Staff details
included in volume continuing until
1948. See **LM&S** [X 480/3]

Cheshire Record Office
1846-1847 Wages book [NPR1/16]
c1926-1941 Staff circulars [NPR2/13]

Derbyshire Record Office
c1909-1924 Reg of workmen, carriage
and wagon depots. Includes some
LM&S. [D3220]

Leicestershire Record Office
1887 Letters re appt A.J. Higginson as
tempy assistant porter Stirchley
[Misc.122]

Public Record Office [Rail 410]
1830-1848 Salary alterations book [1876]
1831-1863 Salaried officers [1871]
Index to 1871 [1872]
1832-1856 Salaried officers Southern
Division [1869]
1837-1871 Reg of staff [1805]
1838-1845 Salaried officers North East
Division [1870]

LONDON AND NORTH WESTERN
RAILWAY (Cont)
Public Record Office [Rail 410] (Cont)
1838-1878 Permanent salaried officers
[1854]
1838-1923 **Cromford & High Peak Rly**,
misc papers inc list of staff employed,
service histories of staff [1309]
1845-1878 Salaried officers Goods dept
[1837]
1847-1927 Chester loco shed [1971]
1850-1901 Coaching, tffc and police
depts [1797-1799]
1852-1876 Rolls of directors and principal
officers [1267]
1852-1878 Reg of staff [1806]
1852-1923 Rolling stock dept, Crewe
[1811]
1854-1922 Bushbury M.P. depot [1834]
1857 Letter from H.Harley [later Secretary
L&NW (1888-91) asking for increase
in salary [1562/2]
1858 Letter from J.Slater, C&W Works,
Saltley, Birmingham, applying for
promotion [1563/13]
1859 Petition from Jacob Crosse, engine
driver, against dismissal through
purchasing a sweep ticket on Chester
Cup races [1533]
1861-1896 Supt's dept [1812 + 1813]
1861-1914 Old Northampton staff regs,
coaching and police depts
[1814 + 1815]
1862 Servants employed on Merthyr,
Tredegar and Abergavenny line
[1567/3]
1862 Corres for Cdr. Risk RN on appt as
Naval Supt, Holyhead, with printed
testimonials [1567/6]
c1862-1905 Camden Goods station
[1904]
1864 Erdington, Stn Master's house
[1173]
1864-1907 Staff book [1874]
1865-1888 Reg of fines [1972]
1865-1920 Broad Street station [1831]
1866-1878 Salaried payment books for
Northampton District [1900 + 1901]
1867-1917 Liverpool Goods depots,
supervising and clerical [1975]
1868-1903 Staff reg [1873]

LONDON AND NORTH WESTERN RAILWAY (Cont)

Public Record Office [Rail 410] (Cont)

1869 Petition from industrialists against removal of Mr.Farr, Goods Manager of Chester and Holyhead branches consequent upon his promotion, as he was such a good servant and their own interests might suffer [1545]

1869-1909 Liverpool Goods depots, supervising and clerical [1973]

1869-1915 Liverpool Goods depots, supervising and clerical [1974]

1869-1920 Liverpool Goods depots, unappointed clerical staff [1979]

1872-1925 Brimswick Goods stn, clerical and wages [1981]

1873-1885 Reg of staff [1807]

1873-1926 Liverpool Goods depots, **former Midland Railway** supervisory and clerical [1978]

1874-1922 Rolls of directors and principal officers [1268]

1875-1911 Coaching and police depts [1802]

1876 Workmens' cottages at St. Helens Jcn [1070]

1876-1920 Liverpool Goods depots, supervising and clerical [1976]

1876-1923 Guards [1828]

1877-1881 Manchester London Road [1830]

1877-1921 Sal staff cards [1890 + 1891]

1877-1929 Alexandra Dock Goods station wages staff [1982]

1879-1893 Reg of staff [1808]

1879-1926 Liverpool Goods depots **former L&Y Rly** supervisory and clerical staff [1977]

c1880-1912 Carriage and goods depts at Broad Street and Shoreditch stns [1985]

1880-1926 Liverpool goods depots unappointed clerical staff [1980]

1882-1926 Wages staff cards [1892]

1894-1899 Punishments book [1823]

1894-1910 Coaching, police, tffc etc depts [1803 + 1804]

1897-1922 Birmingham New St reg [1835]

1897-1922 Allowances and gratuities to salaried officers and staff [1889]

1898-1903 Caution/suspension book [1826]

LONDON AND NORTH WESTERN RAILWAY (Cont)

Public Record Office [Rail 410] (Cont)

1898-1911 Caution/suspension book, joint staff [1827]

1899-1901 Suspension book [1824]

1902-1910 Coaching dept [1800]

1902-1910 Tffc, police and telegraph depts of **LNW** and **Ashby & Nuneaton** railways [1801]

1903-1923 Supt of Line, Euston to Crewe [1809 + 1810]

1907 Album of signatures of staff which accompanied an illuminated address thanking the Directors for guaranteeing the benefits of the superannuation fund [1219]

1910-1913 Salaries alterations book [1877]

1911 Illuminated address to Charles Byrom on his leaving the Swansea & Central Wales Division [1360]

Salaries alterations books
1911-1914 [1878]
1914-1921 [1879]
1916-1921 [1883]
1919-1927 [1882]
1921-1922 [1880 + 1881]
1922-1926 [1884]

1911-1922 Birmingham New St punishment book [1836]

1914-1921 Hotel and refreshment room salaries [1875]

1915-1922 Suspension book [1825]

1915-1922 Wages alterations book [1885]

1917-1920 Staff engagement agreements [1902 + 1903]

1920-1921 Salary list, Penkridge stn tffc dept [1402]

1921 Officers and other staff with their present and proposed positions on the **amalgamation of L&NW** and **L&Y Rlwys** as from 1st Jan 1922 [1897]

1921-1922 Hotel, refreshment room and laundry alteration book [1886]

Caution books

1895-1898 [1816]	1905-1906 [1820]
1898-1900 [1817]	1906-1907 [1821]
1901-1902 [1818]	1922-1924 [1822]
1903-1905 [1819]	

LONDON AND NORTH WESTERN (Cont)
Public Record Office [Rail 410] (Cont)
Registers of salaried staff
Goods dept

1843-1897 [1842]	1856-1918 [1840]
1851-1917 [1839]	1857-1897 [1843]
1855-1917 [1841]	1858-1918 [1838]

Coaching dept

1839-1878 [1844]	1858-1897 [1847]
1856-1917 [1846]	1863-1917 [1845]

Miscellaneous depts

1840-1897 [1850]	1856-1918 [1849]
1840-1917 [1848]	

Indexes
A-K [1851] L-Z [1852] General [1853]

Permanent officers and servants

1833-1857 [1857]	1847-1852 [1858]
1836-1851 [1855]	1852-1860 [1859]
1837-1863 [1856]	1866-1878 [1860]

Permanent officers and servants inc
    staff on **certain North London** and
    **North & South Western Junction
    Rly Co's stations** 1855-1917 [1861]

Permanent officers and servants inc
    staff **transferred from Chester and
    Holyhead** and **Lancaster and Carlisle
    Railways** 1848-1862 [1862]

Indexes to registers of officers and
    servants [1863-1868]

Crewe Works records
AR Series regs
1867-1868 [1905]
1869-1870 [1906]

1872-1884 A-H	[1907]
1872-1884 J-Z	[1908]
1883-1990 A-H	[1909]
1883-1900 J-Z	[1911]
1890-1901 A-I	[1910]
1890-1901 J-Z	[1912]
1901-1911 A-H	[1913]
1901-1911 J-Z	[1914]

AL Series regs
1872-1875 [1915]
1875-1887 [1916]
1887-1898 [1917]

LONDON AND NORTH WESTERN (Cont)
Public Record Office [Rail 410] (Cont)
Crewe Works (Cont)
FR Series regs

1872-1873 [1918]	1874-1875 [1919]
1875-1878 [1920]	1878-1882 [1921]
1882-1887 [1922]	1887-1891 [1923]
1891-1894 [1924]	1894-1898 [1925]
1898-1901 [1926]	1901-1904 [1927]
1905-1908 [1928]	

MR Series regs

1873-1874 [1929]	1874-1876 [1930]
1876-1879 [1931]	1879-1882 [1932]
1882-1885 [1933]	1886-1889 [1934]
1889-1891 [1935]	1892-1895 [1936]
1895-1898 [1937]	1898-1899 [1938]
1899-1901 [1939]	1900-1917 [1945]
1901-1902 [1940]	1902-1905 [1941]
1905-1908 [1942]	1908-1911 [1943]
1911-1913 [1944]	

Alph. regs
1872-1875 [1946]
1899-1912 A-Z [1949]
1908-1922 A-M [1947]
1908-1922 N-Z [1948]
1913-1919 A-Z [1950]
1920 A-Z [1951]

1854-1906 Outdoor depots & stns [1952]
1907-1920 [1953]

Under control of various foremen

1908-1912 [1954]	1912-1914 [1955]
1913-1919 [1957]	1914-1917 [1956]
1919 [1958]	

Manager's reg of staff

1913-1915 [1959]	1915-1918 [1960]
1918-1921 [1961]	1921-1925 [1962]

1908-1913 Locomotive dept [1963]
1915-1928 Tradesmen 21-25 years
    [1964]
1883-1931 Sal staff transferred from
    wages grade [1965]
1914-1920 Tempy staff during war
    [1966]
1914-1918 Tempy staff during war
    [1967]
1911-1919 Register A-I [1968]
1911-1919 Register J-Z [1969]
1920 Register A-I [1970]

LONDON AND NORTH WESTERN (Cont)
Public Record Office [Rail 623]
1862-1897 Staff records.Included in
   Shropshire Union [67 + 68]

**L&NW/FURNESS RAILWAYS JOINT
   COMMITTEE**
Public Record Office [Rail 403]
1899-1906 List of staff [7]

**L&NW/GREAT WESTERN JOINT
   COMMITTEE**
Cheshire Record Office [NPR2/]
1850's-1870's Chester Div. Tffc Dept
   wages and some salaried staff. Inc
   Supt's Office, Chester.[1]
1850's-1870's As above, without Supt's
   office [2]
1880's-1890's As above.[3]
1870's-1890's As above. [4]
1870's-early 1900's As above [5]
1870's-early 1900's As above. [6]
1860's-1890's Shrewsbury Dist sal staff
   reg. Inc Supt's office [8]
1860's-1900's Coaching Dept Chester-
   Holyhead staff reg [10]
1900's-1913 As above, with list of
   pensions allowed and references to
   Supt's [11]
1903-early 1920's Tffc dept wages staff
   reg. Chester and Shrewsbury. [7]

Public Record Office [Rail 404]
1871-1892 Reg joint line staff [177]
1885-1894   ditto   [178]
1894-1897   ditto   [179]
1895-1897   ditto   [180]

**L&NW/MIDLAND RAILWAYS JOINT
   COMMITTEE**
Public Record Office [Rail 406]
1861-1911 Reg coaching & police depts
   Birmingham New St & Derby stns [16]

**LONDON AND SOUTH WESTERN
   RAILWAY**
Originally London & Southampton 1834.
   Name changed to L&SW 1839.
Devon Record Office
1899-1925 Time book with names.
   Stations inc Barnstaple and Exmouth
   [3280B/A6]

LONDON & SOUTH WESTERN RLY (Cont)
Devon Record Office (Cont)
1904-1908 Wages book. Stations include
   Bideford, Barnstaple, Ilfracombe
   [3280B/A2]
1924-1925 As previous item [3280B/A3]

Hampshire Record Office
1841-1861 Diaries of J.D.Blake of
   Romsey and Aldershot (railway
   telegraph clerk) 13 vols [30M73/F1-
   13]

Public Record Office [Rail 411]
1842-1920 Loco dept staff register [665]
1865-1868 Paybook Exeter Goods dept
   [485]
1865-1925 Reg agents incl S.M.'s [498]
1866-1924 Regs Goods dept [517-519]
1870-1924 Regs Loco dept workmen
   [522 + 523]
1871-1929 Loco dept (Western section)
   shed and shop staff [666]
1873-1924 Regs Goods dept clerical staff
   [504 + 505]
1886-1920 Reg Nine Elms weekly salaried
   staff [520]
1887-1897 Reg Devonport station [483]
1889-1896 Fines,drivers & firemen [521]
1889-1907 Reg Godalming station [484]
1903-1917 Loco dept reg of workmen
   [667]
1915-1924 Reg female clerical staff[506]

Cautions and commendations to
   enginemen
c1889-1943 [486]   c1900-1943 [488]
c1891-1937 [490]   c1914-1944 [489]
c1894-1942 [487]

Clerical staff character books
1838-1877 [491] 1859-1920 [494]
1838-1919 [492] 1871-1920 [495]
1839-1920 [493] 1895-1920[496]
1856-1921 [497] [weekly paid]

Salaried staff registers
1841-1921 [499] 1865-1924 [501]
1851-1924 [500] 1873-1924 [502]
1913 Index [503]

LONDON & SOUTH WESTERN (Cont)

Public Record Office [Rail 411] (Cont)

Wages staff registers

1861-1926 [511] 1893-1927 [512]
1865-1924 [507] 1895-1927 [514]
1878-1926 [510] 1896-1927 [515]
1885-1925 [508] 1898-1927 [513]
1887-1926 [509] 1899-1927 [516]

Regs of workmen at various LC&W depots

1844-1890 [524] 1881-1890 [528]
1863-1894 [530] 1886-1890 [529]
1864-1877 [525] 1877-1890 [526]
Index to 524+526 [527]

LONDON BRIGHTON AND SOUTH COAST RAILWAY

Formed by union of London & Brighton and London & Croydon Rlys 1846.

Brighton Reference Library

Unpublished biographies of LB&SCR staff inc Brighton Works drivers etc.

Eastbourne & District F.H.S.

Index of staff in the Eastbourne area census returns 1841 to 1881.

Public Record Office [Rail 414]

Traffic staff appointments

1837-1861 [770] 1837-1864 [771]
1838-1869 [772] 1838-1874 [773]
1838-1879 [774] 1838-1884 [775]
1846-1894 [777] 1846-1898 [778]
1847-1901 [779] 1851-1904 [780]
1856-1907 [781] 1856-1912 [782]
1864-1917 [783] 1866-1921 [784]
1884-1889 [776]

Loco Dept (Brighton Section) staff regs

1854-1878 Volume 1 [863]
1868-1892 Volume 3 [864]
1876-1892 Volume 2 [865]
1891-1909 Volume 6 [866]
1893-1898 Volume 4 [867]
1897-1902 Volume 5 [868]
1907-1913 Volume 7 [869]
1912-1919 Volume 8 [870]
1913-1919 Volume 9 [871]
1918-1936 Volume 10 [872]

1852-1905 Portsmouth joint staff [785]
1854-1905 Willow Walk and Newhaven Harbour [786]

LONDON, BRIGHTON & SOUTH COAST (Cont)

Public Record Office [Rail 414] (Cont)

1854-1910 Willow Walk and Newhaven Hbr and Portsmouth joint staff [787]
1855-1923 Portsmouth joint staff appointed 1855-1920 [789]
1856 Traffic staff histories based on questionnaire relating to staff appointed 1836-1854 [767]
1858-1883 Reg of appointments [760]
1861-1922 Willow Walk and Newhaven Hbr and Portsmouth joint staff [788]
1862-1863 Optg staff, offences etc [759]
1864-1879 Reg of salaried staff apptd 1836-1879 [768]
1871 Dec 31 Staff reg, all depts [763]
1873-1874 Job applns, L&C dept Brighton Works [753]
1873-1925 Clerical staff appointed 1873-1923 [790]
1875 Job applns L&C dept Brighton Works [755]
1877 Dec 31 Staff reg, all depts [764]
1880-1902 Reg of salaried apptd 1839-1902 [769]
1881 Dec 31 Staff reg, all depts [765]
1882 Job applns L&C dept Brighton Works [754]
1882-1908 Staff in Loco Supt's dept, mainly at Brighton [752]
1883-1904 Reg of appointments [761]
1891 Dec 31 Staff reg, all depts [766]
1905-1913 Reg of appointments [762]
1909-1922 Memoranda of meetings between Loco Engineer and staff delegates [758]
1914-1920 Staff of all depts on active service 1914-1918 [791] Index [792]

LONDON CHATHAM AND DOVER RAILWAY

Originally East Kent Rly 1853. Name changed to LC&D 1859. Leased to SE&C Rly Co's Managing Cttee 1899.

Public Record Office [Rail 415]

c1859-1910 Secretary's dept staff in Audit Office [104]
1860-1881 Staff at Longhedge Works and outstations [109]
1864-1918 Staff at Longhedge Works and outstations [110]

LONDON CHATHAM & DOVER (Cont)
Public Record Office [Rail 415] (Cont)
1898 Loco, Carriage and Marine depts
staff [173]

**LONDON MIDLAND AND SCOTTISH
RAILWAY**
Bedfordshire Record Office
1921-1948 Potton station. Book
concerning staff with details of
hours worked, payments to men on a
daily basis, income tax, signatures for
documents etc., issue of clothing,
staff changes etc. [X 480/3]

Public Record Office [Rail 1057]
1841-1899 Biographical material re Sir
Richard Moon who succeeded Admiral
Moorsom as Chairman, LNWR in 1861
[3329]
1857-1899 Biography of John Diggle,
clerk, Bolton & Leigh etc Railways,
among other documents [3390]
c.1873 Lord Wolverton (George Carr Glyn)
Biographical material [3335]
1884-1947 W.E. Gladstone Fund for
Indigent Locomen. Donation of
£500 for relieving long-service
drivers Euston-Crewe-Chester.
Grants etc. [3298]
1890-1931 File inc home addresses of
Directors [3318]
1918-1948 Board members with details of
remuneration etc [3319]
1923 Papers re death of Sir William
Thorburn March 18: applns for post of
consulting surgeon; appt of Mr.V.
Warren Low, May 1923 [3302]
1923-1939 Directors' remuneration;
papers concerning individual Directors
[3322]
1923-1946 File inc lists of Directors
appointments and retirements
[3324]
- Similar to 3324 inc details of deaths
[3325]
1923-1945 Similar to 3324 and 3325,
with details of committee
membership [3326]
1924-1946 Biographical details etc of
Directors [3333]

LONDON MIDLAND & SCOTTISH (Cont)
Public Record Office [Rail 1057] (Cont)
1925-1939 Various details re Directors inc
list of former LNW Chairmen with
periods in office [3327]
1929-1946 William Whitelaw (LNER),
biographical material - an LMS file
[3332]
1945-1948 Directors' names, ages etc
[3323]

**Personal files relating to individual
Directors:**
- Lord Lawrence of Kingsgate [3342]
- George Macpherson [3344]
- W.E. Dorrington [3379]
1909-1946 Major J.A.W.O.Torrens (with
papers relating to appointment of Sir
Thomas Somerset as Chairman,
Northern Counties Committee, and
filling of other vacancies) [3358]
c1911-1912 Lord Stalbridge [3353]
1911-1923 Sir Gilbert Claughton [3378]
c1919-1934 Sir Thomas Williams [3363]
c1922-1943 Sir Ralph Glyn [3381]
c1924 Charles Cropper [3377]
c1926-1929 Charles Booth [3373]
1927-1944 Lord Jessel of Westminster
[3389]
c1928-1930 F.H. Wedgwood [3360]
c1928-1935 Lord Knutsford [3341]
c1928-1943 Gen. Sir H.A. Lawrence
[3343]
c1929-1929 Sir Edwin Stockton [3355]
c1929-1940 Charles Ker [3340]
c1930-1936 Gustav Behrens [3371]
c1930-1940 W.L. Hichens [3387]
c1930-1944 Viscount Runciman [3351]
1931-1949 E.B. Fielden [3380]
1932-1933 A.H. Wiggin [3362]
c1933-1937 Sir Arthur Rose [3349]
1934-1947 Sir Robert Greig [3384]
1934-1951 Sir Francis Joseph [3388]
1935 F.J. Ramsden [3348]
c1935-1940 Sir Alan Anderson [3368]
c1935-1942 Sir John Beale [3370]
1937 Douglas Vickers [3359]
1937 J. Bruce Ismay [3386]
1937-1945 Lord Wigram [3361]
c1937-1946 Sir Robert Burrows [3375]
1937-1947 Sir William V. Wood [3364]
1938 J. Hamilton Houldsworth [3385]
1939 J.W. Murray [3345]

LONDON MIDLAND & SCOTTISH
RAILWAY (Cont)
Public Record Office [Rail 1057] (Cont)
1939-1944 Sir Thomas Brocklebank [3374]
c1939-1946 Sir Thomas Royden [3350]
c1939-1947 Earl Peel [3346]
1940 Sir Ian Bolton [3372]
c1940-1944 Lord Aldenham [3366]
c1940-1945 A.E. Pullar [3347]
1941 D.M. Evans Bevan [3369]
1941-1943 Sir Guy Granet OBE [3383]
1942-1945 G.R.T. Taylor [3357]
1943 Alexander Murray Stephen [3354]
1943-1944 Richard F. Summers [3356]
1943-1944 Lt.Col. F.M.G. Glyn [3382]
1945 Sir Alan Anderson CBE [3367]
1945-1947 Lord Woolton of Liverpool [3365]
1946 Sir Ewart Smith [3352]
1947 Sir Robert Burrows (with photos of naming ceremony at Preston of Royal Scot loco 6135 'The East Lancashire Regiment') [3376]

Scottish Record Office [BR/LMS/15]
1925-1928 Staff book Polmadie shed [19]
1926-1931 Workmen St.Rollox Works [23]
1930 Staff Goods dept Greenock [18]
1937 C.M.E's dept [C&W], District Foremen, Works Supt's and Outdoor Assistants [17]
c1945-1946 Incomplete reg coach and wagon works [25]

Scottish Record Office
A G Dunbar Collection [GD344]
1870-1931 Staff book Balornock shed includes Cal Rly [2/38]
1910-1957 Staff seniority list Yoker shed, inc Cal Rly and BR (ScR) [2/39]
1922-1926 Staff book Polmadie shed includes Cal Rly [2/46]

LONDON MIDLAND & SCOTTISH AND
LONDON & NORTH EASTERN
JOINT COMMITTEE
Public Record Office [Rail 417]
1891-1938 Staff register of traffic and parcels depts at Leeds New Station [16]

LONDON TILBURY AND SOUTHEND
RAILWAY
Incorp 1862. To Midland Rly 1912.
Public Record Office [Rail 437]
Staff registers

1861-1901 [52]	1871-1916 [54]
1897-1901 [48]	1875-1889 [46]
1902-1910 [49]	1877-1910 [53]
1909-1916 [45]	1885-1923 [55]#
1910-1915 [50]*	1888-1909 [44]
1915-1920 [51]*	1889-1897 [47]

* From 1912 relates to **Mid.Rly LT&S sec**
# Manager's, Passenger traffic outdoor staff and Train Working offices

MANCHESTER AND MILFORD RAILWAY
Incorp 1860. Leased to GWR 1906.
Vested in GWR 1911.
Public Record Office (Rail 456)
Oct 1873 List of staff [13]
Aug 1880 List of staff [13]
1905-1911 Pensions and gratuities to staff after amalgamation with GWR [15}

MANCHESTER SHEFFIELD AND
LINCOLNSHIRE RAILWAY
Formed 1846 by amalgamation of five companies. Further amalgamation 1847. Renamed Great Central 1897.
Public Record Office [Rail 463]
From 1847 Accountant's staff regs [305+306]
and
MS&L Rly and Canal general staff books [307-312]
1847-1897 Staff book Audit Office [210]
1851-1876 Reg Audit Office [210]
1852-1917 Reg Acct's Office vol 4 [219]
1853-1905 Staff book Audit Ofice [218]
1855-1857 Paybill Hazlehead Bridge stn [174]
1862 Accountant's personal staff [313]
1862-1912 Reg of principal staff [224]
1863 Acct's personal staff [314 + 315]
1863-1914 Reg of Officers [222]
1864-1902 Reg Goods Audit Office [212]
1864-1913 Reg Goods Audit Office [213]
1864-1921 Reg Acct's Office vol 1 [214]
1869-1906 Reg Sheffield, including diary of events 1879-1892 [249]
1869-1920 Reg Acct's Office vol 5 [220]
1869-1926 Reg Acct's Office vol 6 [221]

MANCHESTER SHEFFIELD & LINCOLNSHIRE RAILWAY (Cont)
Public Record Office [Rail 463] (Cont)
1870-1894 Staff reg Trafford Park loco depot [177]
1870-1914 Reg in sections [226]
1870-1925 Reg Acct's dept, general office [225]
1876-1898 Reg Audit office [211]
1876-1920 Reg of Officers [223]
1895-1957 Rent roll book [176] * *
* * From 1923 relates to **L&NER** and from 1948 to **BR (ER)**
1900-1912 Reg Accountant's office vol 2 [215]
1900-1925 Reg Accountant's office vol 3 [216]
1881-1896 Reg, joint agencies [247] Index [248]
For later volumes see **Great Central Rly**

The following are staff registers:
1845-1875 vol 3 [229] Index [230]
1851-1924 vol 8 [239] Index [240]
1862-1881 vol 5 [233] Index [234]
1870-1875 vol 4 [231] Index [232]
1874-1881 vol 6 [235] Index [236]
1881-1889 vol 7 [237] Index [238]
1888-1892 vol 9 [241] Index [242]
1892-1896 vol 10 [243] Index [244]
1896-1910 vol 11 [245] Index [246]
1852-1901 Joint Lines [227] Index [228]
For continuation see **Great Central Rly**

MANCHESTER SOUTH JUNCTION AND ALTRINCHAM RAILWAY
Incorp 1845 by amalgamation of Manchester & Birmingham and Sheffield, Ashton-under-Lyne & Manchester. Further amalgamations 1846 to form Manchester Sheffield & Lincolnshire. Sold to L&NW 1847.
Public Record Office [Rail 465]
1892-1893 Driver's log [57]
Feb 1904 Presentation to R.H.Brown on retirement as Secretary & Manager [53]
1905-1908 Wages bills, Sale and Ashton-on-Mersey station [55 + 56]

MARYPORT AND CARLISLE RAILWAY
Incorp 1837.
Cumbria Record Office (Carlisle)
1864-1906 Plans, including workmen's cottages Ca/E4/

MARYPORT & CARLISLE (Cont)
Cumbria Record Office (Carlisle) (Cont)
1867-1910 Memo's including deduction of fines from employees' pay [DX/485/1-3]
1880,1885 Testimonials given to William Bewley of Maryport [DX/1008/1]
1903 Election of John Musgrave of Wasdale Hall as Director [D/Mg/57/1]

Public Record Office [Rail 472]
1861-1912 Accidents and offences, drivers and firemen [51]
1878 Deed of contract for erection of 12 cottages at Currock Jcn [36]
1891-1910 Wages sheets (10 files) [50]

MERSEY RAILWAY
Incorp 1866 as Mersey Pneumatic Rly. Name changed 1868.
Public Record Office [Rail 475]
1885-1907 Reg Birkenhead Cen stn [41]

MIDDLESBOROUGH AND GUISEBOROUGH RAILWAY
Incorp 1852. Vested in Stockton & Darlington 1858.
Public Record Office [Rail 483]
1853 Memorial from shareholders etc recommending Geo Page as first Station Master Guiseborough [26]

MIDDLESBOROUGH & REDCAR RAILWAY
Incorp 1845. Leased to Stockton & Darlington 1847. Vested in S&DR 1858.
Public Record Office [Rail 484]
1845-1857 Staff returns etc [33]
1846 Workmen attending opening ceremony, with innkeeper's accounts for food and liquor [46]
1846-1847 Directors' attendances and fees [39]
1847 Platelayers monthly time and wages [40]

MIDLAND RAILWAY
Formed 1844 by amalgamation of North Midland, Midland Counties and Birmingham & Derby.
Bristol Reference Library
1914-1919 Roll of Honour, Bristol Goods stn staff, First World War, 206 names

MIDLAND RAILWAY (Cont)
Cumbria Record Office (Carlisle)
1899 Scotby, plan of cottages
(S/RD/BB/3/2/31)
1906 Robert Richardson, appointment as
assistant porter Ormside [DX/1122/1]

Derby Local Studies Library
1870 Public dinner for W.E. Hutchinson
1874 Public dinner for W.P. Price

Derbyshire Record Office
1875-1937 Records of St. Christopher's
Railway Servants Orphanage, Derby
[D3320]. *Due to the recent and
personal nature of details in these
records they are not at present open to
public inspection. Record Office staff
will, however, examine them for a fee
on behalf of bona fide relatives.
Application should be made to the
Archivist with as much information as
possible. A comprehensive article on the
history of the Orphanage appears in
Volume 12 (1903) of* The Railway
Magazine.

The following three entries include
LM&SR and **BR (LM Region)**
c1900-c1970 Litchurch Lane, Derby,
C&W Works personnel [D3220]
c1900-c1970 Siddals Road, Derby,
Locomotive Works personnel [D3220]
c1914-c1950's C&W dept personnel
[D3220]

Leicestershire Record Office
c1895-1912 Reg, Loughborough
[DE2503/3]

Public Record Office [Rail 491]
N.D. Pedigree lists [1040 + 1041]
c1833-1888 Sheffield stn [1073 + 1074]
1859-1866 Staff list [1039]
1860-1875 Mineral Office reg [1029]
1864-1873 Loco dep foremen, clerks,
time-keepers etc [1067]
1866-1901 Misc letters inc app'tment and
resignation of W.H. Hodges, Acct [966]
1868-1873 Staff reg [1032]

MIDLAND RAILWAY (Cont)
Public Record Office [Rail 491] (Cont)
The following * are staff registers dating
from c1870 :-
* Goods Manager St. Pancras [969 + 970]
* St. Pancras carting, stable and market
staff [971 + 972]
* Carting depots, Castle & Falcon and
Borough Receiving Offices [973]
* Somers Town [974 + 975]
* Whitecross Street, Victoria Docks,
Poplar and Bow [976]
* London carting depots [977]
* London commercial wages staff [978]
* London outlying depots [979]
* London District, medium and small
stations [980]
* Victoria Docks and Poplar [981]
* Whitecross Street [982]
* City depot [983]
* Goods Manager's Office Bow [984]
* Goods Manager's Office Liverpool
Victoria [985]
1870-1876 Joint staff lists [1034]
1871-1879 Coaching dept [1024]
1871-1877 New appointments [1015]
1872-1892 Loco dept [1068]
1873-1911 Telegraph dept personal staff
[988-990]
1874-1919 Staff record G. Simmens
[1081]
1875-1895 Mineral Office reg [1030]
1876-1892 Joint staff lists [1035]
1876-1907 Derby [1001]
1876-1908 Burton [999]
1876-1908 Gloucester, Bath, Bristol
[1002]
1876-1908 Leeds [1004]
1876-1908 Leicester [1005]
1876-1908 Masborough, Staveley and
Chesterfield [1006]
1876-1908 Nottingham and Beeston
[1007]
1876-1908 St. Pancras [1008 + 1009]
1876-1908 Saltley and Birmingham
[1010]
1876-1908 Sheffield [1011]
1876-1908 Skipton, Keighley, Shipley and
Hellifield [1012]
1876-1908 Toton [1013]
1876-1908 Trent, Lincoln, Mansfield and
Westhouses [1014]
1877-1882 New appointments [1016]

MIDLAND RAILWAY (Cont)
Public Record Office [Rail 491] (Cont)
1877-1911 Telegraph dept station staff [991 + 992]

1880-1908 Kettering, Northampton, Luton etc [1003]

1880-1908 Cudworth, Sheepridge, Eckington etc [1000]

1880-1908 Goods g'rds [1022 + 1023]

1881-1898 Coaching dept [1025]

1882-1890 New appointments [1017]

1890-1897 New appointments [1018]

1892-1909 Loco dept s'visors, clerks, pupils, draughtsmen, photographers, stewards, cooks, messengers etc [1069]

1893-1906 Joint staff lists [1036]

1895-1921 Mineral Office reg [1031]

1896-1921 Clerical staff fines, District Comm Mgr's Office Derby [987]

1897-1900 New appointments [1019]

1897-1911 Birmingham New St joint stn [997]

1897-1916 Wages staff fines, District Comm Mgr's office Derby [986]

1897-1922 Loco dept salaries [1070 + 71]

1878-1911 Bristol joint station [998]

c1890-1931 Bromsgrove wagon works [1072]

1899 -1902 Staff reg [1033]

1899-1907 Sup'tendent's dept [994]

1899-1908 Coaching dep [1026 + 27]

1901-1909 Dist. Supt's personal staff [995 + 996]

1901-1922 Pedigree book [1063]

c1901-1924 Sheffield Goods station and depots [1075]

1901-1949 Alterations book [1064]

1902-1908 Marshalling staff [1028]

1902-1913 New appts Derby Dist [1020]

1906-1911 Telegraph and tffc branch [993]

1906-1920 Joint staff lists [1037]

1906-1920 Burton/Ashby Light Rly [1038]

1906-1930 Additional appointments [1021]

1908 Henry Vardy's leave entitlement [1077]

c1912 Goods stns - numbers of staff, local demand for labour etc. [1066]

1914 Staff on salary list [1076]

-1916 Reg Loco dept Dist staff [1080]

See **Unclassified items** page 57

MIDLAND AND GREAT NORTHERN RAILWAY JOINT COMMITTEE
Eastern & Midlands Rly incorp 1882 by amalgamation of three companies in Norfolk. Acquired by Midland and Great Northern Railways 1893 and managed by committee.
Leicestershire Record Office
1881 Letter of appointment G.A.Huckle tempy assistant porter Tydd St.Mary [C/1952/118]

Public Record Office [Rail 487]
1879-1893 Reg Eastern Section [115]

1917-1921 Cleaners timebook, Melton Constable loco depot [78]

1917-1921 Drivers & firemens timebook Melton Constable loco depot [79]

1937-1938 Drivers & firemens timebook Melton Constable loco depot [80]

MIDLAND AND SOUTH WESTERN JUNCTION RAILWAY
Formed 1884 by amalgamation of Swindon, Marlborough & Andover and Swindon & Cheltenham Extension.
Public Record Office [Rail 489]
1891-1921 Reg L&C dept [21]

MONMOUTHSHIRE RAILWAY AND CANAL
Incorp 1792 (canal) and 1845 (railways). Amalgamated with GWR 1880.
Public Record Office [Rail 500]
Items indicated * are petitions or memorials to the Railway Board

1801* G. Harris for wage advance [43]

1819* H. Howell for a house [43]

1822* J. Howells for a house [43]

1824* Carpenters for wage rise [43]

1824* Labourers for wage rise [43]

1827* T.Jones for a house [43]

1827* W.Williams for a house [43]

1827* J. Parry for a house [43]

1827* W.Jones for a house [43]

1843* Blocklayers re wage cuts [43]

1854* Firemen for wage rise [43]

1854* S.Thomas re contract [43]

1857 Indian Mutiny victims, relief fund subscription lists [57]

1863* G. Hadden re accusations against his character [43]

1864* Guards re extra pay [43]

MONMOUTHSHIRE RAILWAY AND CANAL (Cont)

Public Record Office [Rail 500] (Cont)

1864* Guards re low pay and lack of prospects [43]

1864* Guards re non-receipt of wage increase and giving notice [43]

1864* Guards Gidding & Shoebridge re dismissal arising from previous item [43]

1865 Appl'ns for transfer clerk [65]

1866 Appl'ns for accountant [66]

1870 Loco foremen & drivers, statements of income for tax purposes [67]

1870-1871 Requests for pay rises [68]

1871* Workmen for more pay, less hours [43]

1872 G. Harrison relinquishment of duties [74]

1875 T.D.Roberts appointed Engineer [80]

NEATH AND BRECON RAILWAY

Incorp 1862 as Dulas Valley Mineral Rly. Name changed to N&B 1863. Amalg with Swansea Vale & Neath & Brecon Junction Rly 1869.

Public Record Office [Rail 505]

1903-1920 Reg tfc staff [13]

See GWR amalg lines pages 30 and 31

NEWCASTLE AND DARLINGTON JUNCTION RAILWAY

Incorp 1842. To York & Newcastle 1846. To York, Newcastle & Berwick 1847. To NE Rly 1854.

Public Record Office [Rail 772]

1847-1848 Paybill book, Richmond, Thirsk and Malton, Boroughbridge and Bedale branches [121]

NEWCASTLE-UPON-TYNE AND CARLISLE RAILWAY

Incorp 1829 (horsepower only). Use of locos auth 1835. Amalgamated with North Eastern Rly 1862.

Public Record Office [Rail 509]

1845-1848 Newcastle wages book [96]

1860-1862 Alston Branch paybills [128+129]

N.D. List of salaries [58]

NEWPORT, ABERGAVENNY AND HEREFORD RAILWAY

Incorp 1846

Gwent County Record Office

1847-1860 Reg of wills, probates etc. [D3145.1]

NORTH & SOUTH WESTERN JUNCTION RAILWAY

Incorp 1851. Leased to L&NW, Midland and North London 1871 and managed by committee.

Public Record Office [Rail 521]

1883-1916 Staff agreements [19]

NORTH BRITISH RAILWAY

Incorp 1844

Cumbria Record Office (Carlisle)

1864-1887 Plans, including houses (Ca/E4/)

1922-1948 Carlisle Loco dept LDC mins [DX/932/1-2]

Scottish Record Office [BR/NBR/4]

1850 List of salaried officers [1]

The following * are staff books

1880-1912* Location unspecified [29]

1920-1926* Stations A to L [23]

1920-1926* Stations M to Y [24]

1865-1914* Borders and Carlisle [167]

1872-1920* [168]

1885-1933* [169]

1888-1921* [170]

1883-1916* J&P Cameron [30]

1916-1925* [31]

1919-1922* Central District [33]

1919-1925* [32]

1919-1933* [34]

1920-1927* Central & Southern Secs [5]

1911-1920* Dumbarton/Balloch Joint [175]

1911-1919* Dundee/Arbroath Joint [173]

1919-1928* Dundee/Arbroath and Dumbarton/Balloch Joint [174]

1909-1919* Eastern District [35]

1893-1898* Eastern Section [135]

1898-1908* [136]

1907-1916* [137]

1911-1943* [138]

1914-1931* [139]

1873-1876* Eastern & Southern Secs [140]

1874-1889* [141]

NORTH BRITISH RAILWAY (Cont)
Scottish Record Office (BR/NBR/4) (Cont)
1874-1915* [142]
1899-1933* [143]
1900-1935* [144]
1907-1946*Goods dept clerical [145]
1912-1946* Eastern & Southern Secs
  Passenger dept [146]
1916-1920* Eastern & Southern Secs
  [147]
1919-1931* [148]
1886-1923* Edinburgh Dist [133]
1891-1935* Goods [134]
1863-1921* Edinburgh & Leith stns [191]
1872-1921* Edinburgh, Lothians and
  Borders stations [193]
1920-1926* Engrs, Loco, Marine depts
  [21]
1927-1935* [22]
1909-1919* Fife District [48]
1919-1922* [49]
1920-1927* Fife & Northern Secs [20]
1873-1878* Fife & Northern Secs and
  sundries [98]
1873-1898* [99]
1893-1900* General offices, Loco etc
  [176]
1899-1911* [177]
1911-1916* [178]
1919-1930* [179]
1893-1922* Goods guards etc [183]
1891-1928* Goods handling staff [182]
1844-1862* Guaranteed officers,Head
  Office and stations [189]
1820-1926* Head and Dist offices [17]
1909-1919* [52]
1917-1923* [53]
1926-1933* [18]
1934-1936* [19]
1919-1926* High Street station [41]
1890-1922* Joint lines [171]
1881-1921* [172]
1910-1919* [50]
1919-1921* [51]
1881-1928* Joint lines, Supt's
  offices etc [184]
1885-1945* Loco Supt's staff [180]
1909-1919* Monkland District [37]
1874-1915*Monkland & West Highland
  Sections [116]
1875-1922* [119]
1867-1873* Northern Section [13]
1873-1894* [14]
1873-1915* [100]

NORTH BRITISH RAILWAY (Cont)
Scottish Record Office (BR/NBR/4) (Cont)
1877-1892* [102]
1891-1927* [105]
1893-1899* [106]
1898-1915* [15]
1899-1908* [107]
1904-1927* [108]
1908-1916* [109]
1914-1919* [16]
1916-1920* [110]
1919-1931* [111]
1919-1933* [47]
1919-1945* [46]
1881-1920* Northern Sec and Sundries
                              [103]
1881-1922*   ditto   [104]
1875-1892* Northern Sec, Head office
  etc [101]
1903-1919* Northern and Southern Dist
  [45]
1910-1936* Secretary's dept [25]
1909-1919* Sighthill, High Street and
  Queen Street stations [40]
1919-1924* Sighthill and Queen St [42]
1849-1877* Southern Section [149]
1867-1873* [1]
1873-1887* [2]
1873-1902* [150]
1875-1892* [151]
1880-1919* [152]
1880-1922* [153]
1888-1915* [3]
1888-1927* [151]
1892-1899* [155]
1892-1920* [156]
1892-1928* [157]
1893-1935* Southern Sec Goods dep
  [158]
1895-1933* Southern Section [159]
1898-1929* [160]
1899-1916* [161]
1901-1940* Optg dept [162]
1906-1943* Southern Section [163]
1907-1940* Optg dept[164]
1908-1945* Southern Section [165]
1912-1940* [166]
1915-1920* [4]
1916-1921* [36]
1870-1896* Sundries [26]
1897-1920* [27]
1912-1919* [28]
1894-1927* Supt's office etc [181]
1867-1874* Western Section [6]

NORTH BRITISH RAILWAY (Cont)
Scottish Record Office (BR/NBR/4) (Cont)
1872-1888* [112]
1872-1902* [113]
1873-1876* [114]
1874-1892* [7]
1874-1915* [115]
1875-1884* [117]
1875-1892* [118]
1881-1892* [121]
1883-1926* [122]
1886-1920* [123]
1888-1926* [124]
1888-1928* [125]
1892-1896* [126]
1892-1914* [8]
1896-1902* [127]
1909-1919* [43]
1916-1920* [9+10]
1916-1931* [131]
1919-1922* [38]
1919-1922* [44]
1919-1933* [39]
1920-1927* [11+12]
1879-1892* Western & Southern [120]
1902-1911* Western Sect & Marine
   [128]
1911-1916* [129]
1915-1920* [130]
1918-1931* [132]
1847-1920 Sal staff Loco dept [190]
1869-1924 PerWay etc staff leaving
   service [192]
1870-1922 Weekly staff changes [65-86]
1878-1912 Individual records of members
   of Conciliation Board No.4 [194]
1880-1903 Circulars re appointment of
   Mr. Donaldson, Stn Master Livingston,
   Menstrie & Dalkeith [209]
1885-1904 Dismissals Traffic dept [57]
1889-1891 Staff changes, proposals
   submitted to Board [195]
1894-1920 Staff fined or cautioned [58]
1896-1898 Acct's dept attendance [196]
1905-1914 Wages book East Coast/
   Midland Route conductors, attendants
   etc [198]
-1920 Special staff lists [87]
1920-1948 Weekly staff changes [88]
1921 Gen Mgr's letter book, staff
   classification appeals [187+188]
1922-1946 Reg discipline cases [93]
1923-1934 Office cleaners [56]
1926-1930 Punishments inflicted [59]

NORTH BRITISH RAILWAY (Cont)
Scottish Record Office [BR/NBR/4/] [Cont]
1930-1948 Discipline book [60]
Pre1948 Stations with no goods staff
   [54+55]

Staff cards with details of service
   on NBR and LNER. By surname:
A-G [95]
H-N [96]
O-Y [97]

The following are Time/Rate/Wages books
   for Foremen, Surfacemen, Platelayers
   and Fencers at the locations stated:
1871-1877 Robert Connolly, Calvenbank
   and Rawyards [215+216]
1873-74 / 1888-90 William Dornan,
   Rawyards and Sunnyside [219+220]
1874-1876 / 1883-90 John McKechnie,
   Westcraigs [231+232]
1874-1876 James Trainer, Shettleston
   [250]
1874-1877 Robert Marshall, Westcraigs
   [243]
1875-1876 John Morgan, Rawyards [245]
1875-1876 William Withington,
   Coatbridge Sunnyside [251]
1876-1878 Bernard O'Neil, Sunnyside
   [247]
1876-1882 Denis Martin, Leaend
   [237+238]
1877-1879 Patrick Curran, Parkhead
   [218]
1877-1879/1889-1895 Will Marshall,
   Sunnyside and Westcraigs [234+235]
c1877-1888 Charles McCue, Armadale
   [227+228]
1878-1879 John Martin, Sunnyside [239]
1879-1880 David Doyle, Sunnyside [221]
1880-1883 Owen Flynn, Parkhead [222]
1880-1883 Michael McGarry, Bellgrove
   [233]
1881-1883 Daniel Makerel, Whiflet [226]
1882-1883 Andrew Cowie [217]
1882-1885 M.Gilmartin, Easterhouse
   [223]
1882-1885 Charles Martin, Sunnyside
   [236]
1883-1890 John Martin, Whifflet [240]
1883-1893 John Jarvie, Forrestfield [225]
1885-1891 John McIntyre, Easterhouse
   [229]
1885-1892 Thos Colligan, Armadale [214]

NORTH BRITISH RAILWAY (Cont)

Scottish Record Office [BR/NBR/4] (Cont)

1885-1892 Robert Marshall [244]
1885-1892 David Young, Clarkston [253]
1886-1888 John Ross, Sunnyside [248]
1886-1891 George Scott,Westcraigs [249]
1887-1893 William Wotherington [252]
1888-1890 Bernard Grant, Bellgrove [224]
1891-1892 James Martin [241]
1892-1895 John Nimmo [246]
1893-1898 Michael Martin, Sunnyside [242]
N.D. Dennis McClusky, Coatbridge Cen [230]

Scottish Record Office
A G Dunbar Collection [GD344]

1871-1930 Staff book Kipps shed inc **LNER** [2/36]
1880-1932 Staff book Parkhead and Burnbank sheds, inc **LNER** [2/37]
1922-1935 Staff seniority list Polmont shed, inc **LNER** [2/35]

NORTH EASTERN RAILWAY

Created 1854 by amalgamation of various companies.

Darlington Railway Centre & Museum

Pension Society records, Sickness & Assurance Society records (includes constituents and successors)

Public Record Office [Rail 527]

Items indicated ** have been indexed (surnames) by York Family History Society. Copies of the index have been deposited with the PRO [2279]; Town Docks Museum, Hull; Y.A.S. Claremont, Leeds and York F.H.S.
1857-1931 Staff (except footplate) in the Hull area (Dairycoates, Drypool, Botanic Gardens, Hessle, Brough) also Driffield and Bridlington. Listed by grade and rates of pay [2275] **
1861-1927 Enginemen and firemen at Dairycoates depot, Hull. [2272-2274]**
1900-1920 Engine cleaners and shed staff at Hull depots (Dairycoates, Botanic Gardens), also Bridlington, Doncaster and Sheffield. [2276] **

NORTH EASTERN RAILWAY (Cont)

Public Record Office [Rail 527)] (Cont)

1843-1919 Appts and salaries for C&W foremen in workshops (three items) [1897]
1852-1909 Mutual Assurance Fund [2053]
1854 Paybills drivers, firemen, night watchmen etc [1939+1940]
1854-1918 Appts and salaries for Loco foremen and workshops inspectors (four items) [1896]
1855-1919 Appts and salaries for clerical staff and draughtsmen in workshops (six items) [1895]
1855-1920 Staff notices re passes, investment by staff in company shares etc. [2242]
1856-1954 Darlington District staff histories [1951+1952]
1859-1957 Reg staff at Spennymoor [1909]
1862-1897 Darlington District appl'ns for guards, porters jobs [1956]
1862-1922 Hull District histories [1953]
1866-1874 Darlington Section officers salaries [1898]
1866-1948 Spennymoor staff details [1984]
1872-1901 Shildon Works wages regs [1946]
1872-1955 Stn Masters appointments etc [1912+1913]
1874-1881 North Road Works supervisory staff salaries [1941]
1878 Bishop Auckland goods staff [1910]
1879-1899 Shildon wagon builders wages books [1947]
1881-1882 York Carriage Works piece work introduction, loss of 130 jobs [1906]
1882 Dismissals for petty theft [1902]
1882 Validity of drivers verbal dismissal [1903]
1882-1883 Drivers' request for higher pay and uniform [1907]
1884-1924 Pensions book [1938]
1887 Widdrington paybill [1964]
1891-1906 Hull District signalmens' histories [1948]
1894 A guard's rest hours [1908]
1895-1930 Drivers fines [1949]
1898 Darlington D.S.O. paybill [1958]

NORTH EASTERN RAILWAY (Cont)
Public Record Office [Rail 527] (Cont)
1899-1900 Deductions from clerks, ticket collectors etc for the Mutual Assurance Fund [2054]
1902-1912 NER clerical staff [1917]
1903-1927 Southern Div shed staff fines [1962]
1904-1927 Central Division shed staff fines [1961]
1908-1926 Newcastle District, complaints against enginemen [1959]
1908-1932 Byers Green staff details [1984]
1911 Salary and duties of Chemist at Gateshead [1920]
1912 Survey of weekly household budget of senior clerks. Average rates of pay of clerical grades and station masters with cost of living summary 1896-1910 [1921]
1912 Staff employed in loco depots, loco works and docks [1942]
Dec 1912 Officers and stations [2252]
1912-1922 Shildon Works fines [1927]
1913-1916 Requests for pay rises [1925]
1914-1927 Northern Div shed staff fines [1960]
1916 Traffic staff hours & wages [1911]
1916 Tempy female clerical appt's, with summaries of staff from CME's dept in HM service [1926]
1916 Junior clerks candidates [1965]
1920 S.M's salaries and rents by surname
A-D [1930]
E-K [1931]
L-R [1932]
S-Z [1933]
N.D. Fire brigade: poster with names of brigade companies at Newcastle and Gateshead [2258]
N.D. Staff employed at Hull and York [2277]

Public Record Office [Rail 1057]
1856 Fidelity guarantee Henry Casson, horse and corn buyer and supt. [3765]
1886 Fidelity guarantee John Edward MacNay [3765]

NORTH EASTERN RAILWAY (Cont)
Tyne and Wear Archive Service
1907 C.P.Maltby, Newcastle, job appln [1359/1]
1969 Wages sheets East Boldon [1858/15]

NORTH LONDON RAILWAY
Incorp 1846 as East & West India Docks & Birmingham Junction Rly. Leased to and worked by L&NW 1850. Name changed 1853.
Public Record Office [Rail 529]
1854-1895 Staff regs [132-135]
1882-1909 Clerks' agreements [137+138]
1906 Staff reg coaching and police [131]
1907 Staff reg, new entrants [130]
1912-1920 Engagement agreements [136]
See also **L&NW Rly [1861] page** 37

NORTH STAFFORDSHIRE RAILWAY
Inc 1847, composed of three North Staffordshire railways.
Public Record Office [Rail 532]
1847-1922 Reg clerks, Stn Masters etc [67]
1869-1917 Regs tffc dept [58+59]
1870-1923 Regs telegraph dept [60+61]
1873-1923 Regs and index [62-65]
1878-1914 Reg mainly tffc dept [66]

NORTH SUNDERLAND RAILWAY
Incorp 1892. Closed 27 Oct 1951. Company did not pass to British Transport Commission but was managed by Dist. Goods Supt., BR NE Region, Newcastle. **Available for research only with permission of Departmental Record Officer, Dept of Trade & Industry.**
Public Record Office [Rail 533]
1893 A.M.Price application for post of auditor [75]
1931 Financial history of railway with details of staff etc [26]
1931-1948 Staff employed [76]

NORTH UNION

Formed 1834 by amalgamation of Wigan
Branch Rly (1830) and Preston & Wigan
Rly (1831). The first Rly Amalgamation
in the world. Absorbed by L&NWR
1888.

Public Record Office [Rail 534]
1841-1856 Book of Orders to staff
signed by James Chapman, Secretary,
Treasurer and General Supt [29]

NORTHAMPTON AND BANBURY
JUNCTION RAILWAY

Incorp 1863. Sold 1910 to Stratford-upon-
Avon and Midland Junction Rly Co.

Public Record Office [Rail 538]
1861-1866 Corres of T.D. Butler,
contractor's engineer, including
testimonials for post of Asst Engineer
Ceylon Railway [2]

OTLEY AND ILKLEY JOINT LINE
COMMITTEE

Formed 1861 by Midland and North
Eastern Rly Companies and managed by
joint committee.

Public Record Office [Rail 554]
1865-1901 Staff lists [24 + 25]

OXFORD WORCESTER AND
WOLVERHAMPTON RAILWAY

Incorp 1845. Amalg with others to form
West Midland Rly 1860. Amalg with
GWR 1863.

Public Record Office [Rail 558]
1856 Staff reports [32]

PADARN RAILWAY

Gwynned Archives Service
Records re manning etc catalogued as
'Dinorwic Quarry Collection'

PENRHYN RAILWAY

Gwynned Archive Service
Records re manning etc catalogued as
'Penrhyn Quarries Collection'

PONTOP AND JARROW [BOWES]
RAILWAY [JOHN BOWES &
PARTNERS (LTD)]

Tyne and Wear Archive Service
c1875-1951 Workmen's engagement
book with family details etc [1566/1]

PORT TALBOT RAILWAY AND DOCKS

Incorp 1894.

Public Record Office [Rail 574]
1883-1918 Staff reg [13]

RHONDDA AND SWANSEA BAY
RAILWAY

Incorp 1882. Worked by GWR from 1906.

Public Record Office [Rail 581]
1882-1920 General staff book [36]
1882-1922 Staff reg [37]

RHYMNEY RAILWAY

Incorp 1854.

Public Record Office [Rail 583]
All of these are for **LC&W** department
The following are wages books for drivers
and firemen:
1860-1919 [41]
1890-1893 [43]
1893-1896 [44]
1896-1898 [45]
1899-1901 [46]
1902-1904 [47]
1905-1907 [48]
1908-1911 [49]
1911-1914 [50]
1914-1919 [51]
1918-1922 [53]
1919-1922 [42]
1920-1922 [52]

1860-1921 Staff reg [59]
1869-1904 Staff reg [54]
1870-1897 Staff reg [55]
1896-1922 Superannuation allowances
and accidents [61]
1898-1907 Staff reg [56]
1907-1918 Staff reg [57]
1918-1921 Time book [60]
1919-1922 Staff reg [58]

See GWR amalg lines pages 30 and 31

SCOTTISH CENTRAL RAILWAY

Incorp 1845. Vested in Caledonian 1865.

Scottish Record Office [BR/EDP/15/]
1856 Staff book [1]

SCOTTISH MIDLAND JUNCTION RAILWAY

Incorp 1845. Vested in Scottish North Eastern 1856. Vested in Caledonian 1866.

Scottish Record Office
A G Dunbar Collection [GD344]
1855 Forfar stn staff paylist [1/86]

SHEFFIELD DISTRICT RAILWAY

Incorp 1896.
Public Record Office [Rail 611]
1897 Agt with R.E. Cooper and J. Wilson re duties as Engineers [26]
1904-1916 Appt of H. Willmott, General Manager [25]

SHREWSBURY AND HEREFORD RAILWAY

Incorp 1846. Leased to L&NWR, GWR and West Midland Railway companies from 1862 and managed by Shrewsbury & Hereford Joint Committee. Functions taken over 1867 by L&NW and GW Joint Committee. Vested in GW and L&NW companies 1870.
Public Record Office [Rail 617]
1848-1862 Memoranda including list of staff [29]

SHROPSHIRE UNION RAILWAYS AND CANAL

Incorp 1846. Leased to L&NWR 1847.
Public Record Office [Rail 623]
1844-1879 Staff book [66]
1862-1897 Regs & index. These include records of **West London Extn Rly, L&NW Rly,** and **Lancs & Yorks Joint stations** [67+68]

SOMERSET AND DORSET RAILWAY

Formed 1862 by amalgamation of Somerset Central and Dorset Central Railway Companies. Vested in South Western and Midland Railway Companies 1875.
Public Record Office [Rail 627]
1863-1877 Reg of stations and staff [6]

SOMERSET AND DORSET JOINT LINE COMMITTEE

Records of the Joint Committee set up in 1875 to manage the Somerset & Dorset Rly.
Public Record Office [Rail 626]
1877-1928 Staff books [44-47]
1920-1923 Staff at stations etc [48-51]
1926-1927 Staff at stations etc [52+53]

SOUTH DEVON RAILWAY

Incorp 1844. Amalg with GWR 1878.
Cornwall Record Office
Transcripts of PRO items **Rail 630(2+3)**
(see below)

Devon Record Office
Transcripts of PRO items **Rail 630(2+3)**
(see below)

Public Record Office [Rail 630]
The following are in respect of Traffic dept staff and include similar information for **Cornwall Railway**
1873 Establishment reports [2]
1874 Establishment reports [3]

Public Record Office [Rail 631]
1858 Staff establishment on opening of Cornwall Rly [28]
1869-1870 Officers, drivers etc [108]

SOUTH DURHAM AND LANCASHIRE RAILWAY

Incorp 1857. Amalg with Stockton & Darlington 1862.
Public Record Office [Rail 632]
1859-1864 Staff applications etc [61]

SOUTH EASTERN RAILWAY

Incorp 1836. Combined with London Chatham & Dover 1899 to form one Company to be managed by South Eastern & Chatham Managing Committee.
Public Record Office [Rail 635]
1842-1898 Regs Audit office [201-204]
1845-1900 Regs loco depot workmen [307+308]
1845-1905 Reg C&W workmen [309]
1847-1913 Goods staff [306]
1851 Staff book [196]
1855-1888 Eng dept letter book re staff and stores [213]

SOUTH EASTERN RAILWAY (Cont)
Public Record Office (Rail 635) (Cont)
1857-1875 Papers re Continental Agencies at Paris, Brussels, Boulogne and Calais [215]

1860-1877 Reg Wadhurst stn staff [206]

1864-1919 Loco dept reg of enginemen [399]

1868-1920 Regs Bricklayers Arms drivers firemen, cleaners etc [302-304]

c1869-1944 Enginemen, punishments and awards [305]

1889-1896 Reg Deptford High St paybills [197]

Public Record Office [Rail 1057]
1854-1909 Misc papers inc appt of E. M. G. Eddy to Board 1894-1895 and matters re Board 1909 [2934]

SOUTH EASTERN AND CHATHAM RAILWAY CO's MANAGING COMMITTEE
Records of the Committee set up to manage the combined South Eastern and London Chatham & Dover Companies. Although managed by one Committee the two Companies maintained separate identity until they became part of the Southern Railway in 1923.
Public Record Office [Rail 633]
1850-1922 Clerks in Accountant's office Ashford [377]

1853-1924 Reg C&W dept workmen [372+373]

1858-1924 Audit Acct's office staff [375+376]

1860-1913 Workmen at various depots [368+369]

1861-1920 Goods dept appts [358-361]

1865-1924 Reg loco dep workmen [370+371]

c1882-1922 Reg Marine dept staff [379]

1898-1921 Allowances and pensions (various depts inc Coaching, Engineers, LC&W, Goods, Stores, Telegraph, Marine, Parcels, General Offices, Continental and Widows) [442]

From 1899 Staff book (general) with histories of management and clerical staff appointed between 1853-1922 [346]

SE&C RLY MANAGING CTTEE (Cont)
Public Record Office [Rail 633] (Cont)
From 1899 Reg Continental & Marine, with details of staff appointed 1862-1922 [362]

From 1899 Reg of staff, officers and clerks 1900-1911 [363]

1901-1944 Drivers punishments & awards [343-345]

1904 Ashford Works tradesmen [378]

1905-1908 Report and order books [364+365]

1914-1919 Reg works staff [374]

1918-1923 Reg appt's, transfers etc [366]

1920-1923 Allowances and pensions (similar depts to 442) [443]

The following are staff books for the Coaching Department.

From 1899 Stn Masters and London stns: Staff apptd between 1842-1921 [347]

Undated London stns: staff apptd between 1901-1920 [348]

From 1899 Abbey Wood-Chislehurst stns and Dist. Supt's dept: staff apptd between 1859-1920 [349]

Undated Abbey Wood-Chislehurst: staff apptd between 1899-1919 [350]

From 1899 Chipstead-Hayes: staff apptd between 1860-1923 [351]

Undated Chipstead-Gillingham: staff apptd between 1907-1923 [352]

From 1899 Hastings-Newington: staff appointed between 1857-1920 [353]

Undated Hastings-Nutfield: staff apptd between 1888-1919 [354]

From 1899 New Romney-Sidcup: staff apptd between 1858-1924 [355]

Undated Ore-Sydenham Hill: staff apptd between 1899-1919 [356]

From 1899 Sidley-Yalding: staff apptd between 1856-1923 [357]

The following are Goods Dept staff books:

From 1899 Goods Managers, London & SE Section depots: staff apptd between 1861-1920 [358]

From 1899 SE Section, Dist Supts, Chatham Section and Horse depots: staff apptd between 1875-1920 [359]

From 1899 SE Section, inc London: staff apptd between 1872-1920 [360]

SE&C MANAGING CTTEE (Cont)
Public Record Office [Rail 633] (Cont)
From 1899 C&D Section: staff apptd
between 1865-1909 [361]

SOUTH WALES RAILWAY
Incorp 1845. Amalg with GWR 1863.
Public Record Office [Rail 640]
1844-1860 Reg, clerks [55]
1847-1848 Cash book of expenses for
construction of Cockett Tunnel, with
names of labourers etc [52]
1850-1855 Reg clerks [56]
1852-1857 Drivers punishments etc [47]
1853-1861 Board reports and lists of staff
[30]
1864 Staff, all depts [45]

SOUTH YORKSHIRE RAILWAY
Doncaster Central Library
Material is available, accessible only
through Local History Section indexes

SOUTH YORKSHIRE JOINT RAILWAY
Doncaster Central Library
Material is available, accessible only
through Local History Section indexes

SOUTHERN RAILWAY
NOTE: PRO records are produced on
Special Permission only and subject to
an undertaking with regard to use of
information likely to be extracted.
Other staff records, extending beyond
1923, reflecting SR staffing will be
found in L&SW,SE and SE&C
collections.

Hampshire Record Office
1875-1925 Pamphlet re life of a worker
on Southern Railway [72M94/1]

Public Record Office [Rail 651]
1923-1927 Staff history reg of Station
Masters entering service between 1873-
1915 [7]
c1923-1929 Reg Marine dept Dover [10]
c1923-1944 Cautions and commendations
to enginemen [1 + 2]
1925-1947 Brighton Works Smith's Shop
piecework earnings [5]
1926 Nov Staff census [131]
1927-1941 Brighton Works Loco Shops
piecework percentages [6]

SOUTHERN RAILWAY (Cont)
Public Record Office (Rail 651) (Cont)
1933-1937 Monthly salary lists
Southampton + Marine, Jersey,
Guernsey & St.Malo [8]

STOCKTON AND DARLINGTON RAILWAY
Incorp 1821. Amalg with North Eastern
Rly 1863, but retained its own
management until 1870.
Public Record Office [Rail 667]
1821 G. Atkinson appln for Engineer's
post [900]
1822 Wages lists Brusselton and Etherby
quarries [1532]
1824-1830 Accounts for medical services
to workmen etc [1326]
1825 Job applications [948]
c1825 Workmens' fines [956]
1825-1826 Wage lists,loco and tfc[1527]
1825-1843 Leaders tonnage records with
payments to named drivers [with gaps]
[1450-1455]
1825-1849 Letters re Timothy Hackworth,
including his testimonial from Walbottle
Colliery [1158]
1826 Letters from employees: B.Tully,
G. Jackson, J. Stephenson [959]
1829-1842 Tonnage and payment details
inc names of engine drivers and other
staff [1299]
1830 Various, including complaints from
tenant publicans: requests for jobs and
financial help: further letters from J.
Stephenson [1022]
1830 Job applications [1024]
1831 Applications for employment,
cottages and compensation for injury
[1028]
1831-1861 Notes by G. Graham,driver of
engine No.1, also notes on J. Graham
and T. Storey [427]
1832 Job applications [1044]
1835 Job applications [1070]
c1835 Officials, passenger guards [603]
1835-1849 Job applications, inc J. Nevins
later Stn Master, Stockton [1283]
1835-1849 Public complaints re guard
Harland, policeman Scott and J. Nevins
[1244]
1835-1849 Letters re wage rises [1284]
1836 Job applications [1077]
1836-1839 Coach and carrying dept,
names of guards, drivers etc [1304]

STOCKTON & DARLINGTON RAILWAY (Cont)

Public Record Office [Rail 667] (Cont)

c1836-1844 Letters re J. West, agent at Fighting Cocks [1161]

1837 Job applications [1095]

1837-1847 Drivers wage lists [1530]

1837-1848 Staff appln's, leave etc [1286]

1838 Job applications: tenancy of Railway inn at Stockton; staff protests at fines for attending Stockton Races [1104]

1838-1849 Letters from staff replying to allegations of misconduct and inattention to duty [1285]

1839 Letters re staff, inc two from Joseph Nevins and one from Guard Arnott requesting a scarlet coat and a petition for his re-instatement as porter to the Middlesborough coaches [1114]

1839 Fines imposed on engine drivers, guards etc for running too fast, carrying passengers etc [1117]

1839-1842 Paybills for work on Middlesbro' Dock and Railway [445]

1839-1845 Letters re staff in trouble and applications for their jobs [1220]

1840 Job applications [1125]

1840-1841 Fines for indiscipline [484]

1840-1841 Staff pay,Middlesb'gh [1302]

1840-1841 Two paybills [1567]

1840-1845 Shildon Works pay book [432]

1840-1847 Shildon monthly pay [1303]

1840-1847 Monthly pay, police officers, gatekeepers, watchmen [1307]

1840-1847 Monthly pay, Carrying dept [1308]

1840-1847 Monthly pay, Coaching dept [1309]

1840-1847 Monthly pay, Brusselton Bank and Black Boy [1311]

1840-1848 Letters re clerical work at Middlesborough, Stockton and Wilton-le-Wear stations also railway school Waskerley [1287]

1840-1849 Monthly paybills [1426+1427]

1840-1855 Shildon Works salary reg [555]

1841-1845 Public complaints re staff, inc Fighting Cocks [1218]

1842 Paybills, clerks, guards [1288]

1844-1845 Stanhope railway inclines, fortnightly wage lists [1497]

STOCKTON & DARLINGTON RAILWAY (Cont)

Public Record Office (Rail 667) (Cont)

1844-1846 Shildon tunnel signalmen wage lists [594]

1846-1847 Loco expenses, inc drivers names [1305]

1846-1849 Corres from Thos Manton, Chief of Police, including one re Geo Watkinson transported for 14 years for stealing a coat [1248]

1847 Letter John Dixon to John Pease re future employment [1263]

1847-1849 Fines for negligence etc [504]

1849 List of gatekeepers [1291]

1849-1852 Paybill ledger [1425]

1850 Details of cottages at Waskerley and of those adjacent to the various inclines [596]

1852-1864 Paybills [1430-1433]

1853 Letter from J. Nevins seeking job for his son [1163]

1854 Applications for clerks job at Darlington [506]

1854 Wages list, pway staff, carpenters, masons [1498]

1854 Letter Samuel Smiles to Thos McNay re appt to South Eastern Rly [1164]

1854-1855 Appt of W. English as Mineral Supt [1143]

1855 Wage alterations, Goods dept, guards, porters etc [1289]

1856 Fines [1290]

1862 Forty-two collectors' booklets for subscriptions in aid of destitute Lancashire cotton workers, unable to work through shortage of cotton caused by American Civil War [590]

1865 Police & gatekeepers salaries [1499]

1865-1874 Shildon workmen list, inter alia [676]

1867 Paybills Darlington section Way and Works dept [1500]

1867-1868 John Dixon memorial [543]

1869 Thos McNay, obituary [609]

N.D. Drivers and builders of first engines [654]

The following * are memorials and petitions to the Directors

1832* Staff re death of colleague [830]

1843* Re Robert Dalton, Stockton [788]

1843* Re Christopher Day [826]

STOCKTON & DARLINGTON RLY (Cont)
Public Record Office (Rail 667) (Cont)
1844* Gatekeepers re wage cuts [786]
1853* Re fortnightly wage payments [846]
1865* Wagon wrights strike notice [793]
1865* Urging erection of a few cottages near Darlington station [794]
1867* Drivers and firemen resumption of duty after strike [795]
1868* Platelayers re wage increase [798]
1872* Shildon tunnel signalmen re wage increase [820]
1876* Tow Law workmen re houses [822]
N.D.* Darlington carriage works staff re more pay, less hours [801]
N.D.* Kirkby Thore re dismissal of Stn Master [803]
N.D.* Re John West appt to Fighting Cocks [834]
N.D.* Users of Yarm stn re Thos Temple and his wife [835]

STRATFORD UPON AVON RAILWAY
Incorp 1857. Amalg with GWR 1883.
Public Record Office [Rail 675]
1858 Appln's for post of engineer [24]

STRATFORD UPON AVON & MIDLAND JUNCTION RAILWAY
Incorp 1908 as amalg of S-u-Avon Rly, Towcester & Midland Jcn Rly, Evesham, Redditch & S-u-Avon Jcn Rly, and East & West Jcn Rly.
Public Record Office [Rail 674]
1873-1923 Reg of staff (early entries relate to **East & West Jcn Rly**) [11]

STRATHSPEY RAILWAY
Incorp 1861. Worked/leased by GN of S. Vested in GN of S 1866.
Scottish Record Office [BR/STY/4/]
N.D. List of staff and salaries [2]

SWINDON AND CHELTENHAM RAILWAY
Incorp 1881. Amalg with Swindon, Marlborough & Andover as Midland & South Western Jcn 1884.
Public Record Office [Rail 1057]
1884 Apr 12 Report by B.L. Fearnley on the internal workings of various departments, including salaries etc. [322]

SWINDON & CHELTENHAM RLY (Cont)
Public Record Office (Rail 1057) (Cont)
1884-1888 B.L. Fearnley, Gen Mgr appt and termination of service [319]
1885 Agreements etc with J.R. Shopland re appointment as engineer [318]
1874-1887 J.R. Shopland's claims for salary and fees [351]

TAFF VALE RAILWAY
Incorp 1836. Amalg with GWR 1922.
Public Record Office [Rail 684]
The following are registers of Traffic dept uniform staff:
1840-1882 [94]
1882-1891 [95]
1891-1899 [96]
1897-1903 [97]
1903-1908 [98]
1903-1912 [99]
1908-1924 [105]
1911-1915 [100]
1915-1917 [101]
1917-1919 [102]
1919-1920 [103]
1920-1923 [104]

The following are registers of Locomotive dept maintenance staff:
1852-1890 [108]
1855-1890 [109]
1890-1909 [110]
1910-1919 [112]
1910-1920 [106]
1919-1922 [107]

1866-1920 Reg Loco dept Mtce staff, Drivers, Firemen and Passed Cleaners with index [113]
1890-1910 Reg Loco dept Mtce staff Inc Passed Firemen and Cleaners [111]
1864-1904 Reg Goods dept staff [114]
1871-1922 Reg Goods dept staff [115]
1892-1922 Reg retiring allowances [77]
1893-1903 Appln's for pensions [73]
1903-1912 Appln's for pensions [74]
1912-1921 Appln's for pensions [75]
1921-1922 Appln's for pensions [76]
See GWR amalg lines pages 30 and 31.

TEES VALLEY RAILWAY
Incorp 1865. Vested in North Eastern Rly 1882.
Public Record Office [Rail 687]
1865-1870 Paybill book [16]

TRENT VALLEY RAILWAY
Incorp 1845. Sold to London & Birmingham Company 1846.
Public Record Office [Rail 699]
1845-1846 Men and horses employed [5]

VALE OF CLWYD RAILWAY
Incorp 1856. Leased to L&NW 1864. Vested in L&NW 1867.
Public Record Office [Rail 1057]
c1858 Testimonials in favour of John Lloyd's appln to be Stn Master [3774]

VALE OF GLAMORGAN RAILWAY
Incorp 1889. Worked by Barry Rly.
Public Record Office [Rail 1057]
1892 James Bell, appt'd engineer[1014]

VALE OF NEATH RAILWAY
Incorp 1846. Amalg with GWR 1865.
Public Record Office [Rail 704]
1851-1904 Pay bill book for Merthyr Road 1851- 1853 and Llwydcoed,1853-1904 [17]

Public Record Office [Rail 1057]
1859-1868 Misc papers inc lists of officers and clerks [2951]

WATTON AND SWAFFHAM RAILWAY
Incorp 1869. Leased to Great Eastern 1879. Vested in Great Eastern 1897.
Public Record Office [Rail 714]
1875 Paysheets [7]

WEST CORNWALL RAILWAY
Incorp 1846. Leased to GWR, Bristol & Exeter and South Devon 1865. Following amalgamations of Bristol & Exeter and South Devon with GWR, West Cornwall became GWR property in 1878.
Public Record Office [Rail 725]
1833-1851 Edward Austin testimonials [6]

WHITEHAVEN AND FURNESS JUNCTION RAILWAY
Incorp 1845. Amalg with Furness Rly Company 1866.
Public Record Office [Rail 744]
1856 Staff at stations,with grades [9]

WHITLAND AND CARDIGAN RAILWAY
Auth 1869. Vested in GWR 1890.
Public Record Office [Rail 747]
1876 Wages lists, perway, loco, tfc [37]
1883 J.B.Walton appt'd engineer [21]
1877 Wages lists, Cardigan extension [38]

WILTS, SOMERSET AND WEYMOUTH RAILWAY
Incorp 1845. Vested in GWR 1854.
Public Record Office [Rail 750]
1845-1850 Paybill book [14]
1850-1856 Paybill book [15]
1856-1858 Paybill book [16]

WIRRAL RAILWAY
Incorp 1883. Amalg with Seacombe, Hoylake and Dee Side Rly Company 1891.
Public Record Office [Rail 756]
1884-1926 Staff reg [10]
1892-1921 Staff reg Birkenhead Park station committee [11]

WREXHAM AND ELLESMERE RAILWAY
Incorp 1885. Worked by Cambrian Rly.
Public Record Office [Rail 1057]
1898-1901 A.J. Collins appt as engineer; retirement and death of G. Owen [632]

WYCOMBE RAILWAY
Incorp 1846 and leased to GWR. Amalg with GWR 1867.
Public Record Office [Rail 768]
1858-1861 E.F. Murray's letters re his appointment as engineer after Mr. Brunel's death [14]

YORK AND NORTH MIDLAND RAILWAY
Incorp 1836. In 1854 became part of the North Eastern Railway Company.
Public Record Office [Rail 770]
1843-1850 York and Newcastle Central staff [81]
1848 Six paybills, Coaching dept and salaries Secretary's office [77]

YORK AND NORTH MIDLAND RLY (Cont)
Public Record Office [Rail 770] (Cont)
1848 Whitby/Pickering branch staff [79]
1848 Two paybills Normanton [78]
1848 Staff at Beverley, Bridlington, Hull, Driffield & Selby: crew of *Endeavour* at Selby [80]
1852 June Paybills Hull Goods [46]
1855 Stn Masters, Goods Agents and Mineral Agents [66]

Public Record Office [Rail 1057]
1848 Fidelity guarantee Richard Spence, clerk [3765]
1848 Fidelity guarantee Henry Denniss clerk [3765]
1850 Fidelity guarantee Richard Gill, cashier [3765]

YORK NEWCASTLE AND BERWICK RAILWAY
Incorp 1842 as Newcastle & Darlington Junction Rly Coy. Name changed to York & Newcastle 1846. Amalg 1847 with Newcastle & Berwick and name changed to York, Newcastle & Berwick, subsequently part of the North Eastern Railway.
Public Record Office [Rail 772]
1845 Inspector's timebook for Newcastle & Darlington Rly [79]
1845 Testimonial to Henry Tennant, later G.M. North Eastern Railway [99]
1845 Paybills Eng, Loco & Carriage depts Gateshead [106]
1845-1850 Paybills Berwick Dist [123]
1847 Inspector's timebook [60]
1847-1848 Paybill book (Richmond, Thirsk & Malton Boroughbridge and Bedale branches) [121] *
    * Relates to Newcastle and Darlington Junction Railway
1848 Paybook Eng dept [61]
1848 Timebook Eng dept Carlisle branch [77]
1850 Paybill book. Men's time, working and repairing engines [62]
1852-1857 Paybills Bishop Auckland [124]
1858-1860 Paybills Bishop Auckland and Jarrow Dock [125]

YORK NEWCASTLE AND BERWICK RLY (Cont)
Public Record Office [Rail 1057]
1852 Fidelity guarantee James Close, cashier (two agreements with different guarantors) [3765]

UNCLASSIFIED ITEMS

Mr. Frank Cossey
    In-depth studies of railwaymen who were employed by the **Great Northern, Midland** and **Eastern Counties** railways in the Peterborough area have been undertaken by Mr. Cossey, a railway historian, based on the 1851 census and those for 1861-1881. The former includes employees of railway contractors working in the Peterborough area. The studies were published by the Peterborough Museum Society in their journal "Peterborough's Past" in 1982 and 1986 respectively.
    Mr. Cossey has also compiled extensive detailed information on railwaymen who worked in Lincolnshire and Peterborough area from 1851 to 1891.
    In due course his material will be lodged with the Lincolnshire Archives Office, but is not at present accessible to the public. Mr. Cossey is, however, willing to deal with enquiries on receipt of a stamped addressed envelope or two international reply coupons. His address is 16 Elsea Drive, Northorpe, Bourne, Lincolnshire PE10 0HL.

Cumbria Record Office (Carlisle)
1900-1946 Notebook of William Milburn, driver, recording events of his working life (DX1120/3)
Up to 1978 Notebooks of T. Horseman, driver (DX1120/5-6)

Gwynned Archive Service
There are a number of disparate collections which include items containing names and details of railwaymen e.g. papers of Caernarfon station 1850's-1860's, but these are not systematic.

RECORDS FOR NORTHERN IRELAND

Public Record Office of Northern Ireland
A considerable number of collections
are held including the Ulster
Transport Archive. Family History
Items have not yet been indexed, but
material is held for the following
railways:-
Ards [D2353/3, D3505]

Ballycastle [UTA 6]
Ballymena and Larne [UTA 4]
Ballymena and Portrush [UTA 26]
Ballymena, Ballymoney, Coleraine and
Portrush Jcn [UTA 2]
Ballymena, Cushendall and Red Bay
[UTA 5]
Banbridge Extension [UTA 27]
Banbridge Junction [UTA 18]
Banbridge, Lisburn and Belfast [UTA 19]
Belfast and Ballymena [UTA 28]
Belfast and County Down [UTA 20]
Belfast and Londonderry Jcn [UTA 32]
Belfast and Northern Counties [UTA 11]
Belfast, Ballymena and Ballycastle Jcn
[UTA 29]
Belfast Central [UTA 30, D513/1]
Belfast, Holywood and Bangor [UTA 25]
Belfast, Strandtown and High Holywood
UTA 33]

Carrickfergus and Larne [UTA 3]
Carrickfergus Harbour Jcn [UTA 34]
Castleblaney, Keady and Armagh [UTA 35]

Derry Central [UTA 7]
Downpatrick, Killough and Ardglass Light
[UTA 37]
Draperstown [UTA 8]
Dromara Extension [UTA 38]
Dublin and Antrim Jcn [UTA 14, D 2759]
Dublin and Belfast Jcn [UTA 39]
Dublin and Drogheda [UTA 40]
Dundalk and Enniskillen [UTA 41]
Dundalk, Newry and Greenore [UTA 42]
Dungannon and Cookstown [UTA 43]

Public Record Office of Northern Ireland
(Cont)
Enniskillen and Bundoran [UTA 44]

Giant's Causeway, Portrush and Bush
Valley [UTA 45]
Glenarriff Iron Ore Railway and
Harbour [UTA 46]
Great Northern [UTA 23 + 24,D 3465]
Great Northern and Midland [UTA 47]
Great Southern [UTA 48]
Great Southern and Western [UTA 49]

Irish North Western [UTA 50]

Larne and Antrim [UTA 52]
Larne and Ballyclare [UTA 53]
Larne and Carrickfergus [D 162/109]
Letterkenny [D 2684]
Limavaddy and Dungiven [UTA 9]
Londonderry and Coleraine [UTA 1]
Londonderry and Enniskillen [UTA 13]
Londonderry and Larne [UTA 54]
Londonderry and Lough Swilley [UTA 55]

Midland and Great Western [D 2741]

Newry and Armagh [UTA 16]
Newry and Enniskillen [UTA 56]
Newry, Keady and Tynan Light [UTA 57]
Newry, Warrenpoint and Rostrevor
[UTA 15]
Northern Counties [UTA 12, D 1920]
Northern Ireland [UTA 58]

Portadown and Dungannon [UTA 59]
Portadown, Dungannon & Omagh Jcn
[UTA 17]
Portstewart Tramway [UTA 10]

Sligo, Leitrim and Northern Counties
[D 1780, D 1956]

Ulster [UTA 60]

Wyre Tramway [UTA 61]

U.K RAILWAY SHIPPING RECORDS

These are listed here in two categories:
(a) ships owned by railway companies and ships which used company docks
(b) ships owned and operated by companies with railway associations.

(a) Railway Company ships

These records are lodged at the Public Record Office and indexed under the appropriate railway company. Most of them give details of half-yearly agreements, official logs, accounts of voyages and lists of crew members. They are indicated by letter code, class and piece numbers, also name of ship if given.

CHESTER AND HOLYHEAD *[Rail 113]*
1854 *S.S.Hibernia* [53]

FURNESS *[Rail 214]*
1912-1913 [104]

GREAT CENTRAL *[Rail 226]*
1912 *S.S.Dewsbury* and *S.S.Accrington*
 [235]

GREAT EASTERN *[Rail 227]*
1865-1902 [488]
1902-1907 [489]
1907-1913 [490]

GREAT WESTERN *[Rail 264]*
1861-1905 [454]
1906-1910 [455]
1911-1912 [456]

(Associated with I.K.Brunel) *[Rail 1014]*
1843/1844 List of passengers and
 parcels by *S.S. Great Western* between
 England and New York [8/25]

LONDON & NORTH WESTERN *[Rail 410]*
1861-1905 [1983]
1905-1913 [1984]

**LNWR/LANCASHIRE & YORKSHIRE JOINT
 COMMITTEE** [*Rail 405*]
1861-1905 [43]
1906-1913 [44]

LONDON & SOUTH WESTERN *[Rail 411]*
1862-1886 [531]   1902-1905 [534]
1892-1898 [532]   1906-1910 [535]
1898-1900 [533]   1911-1913 [536]
1899-1913 [537*]
 * Joint with L.B.& S.C.

LONDON BRIGHTON & SOUTH COAST
 [Rail 414]
1862 and 1892-1902 [795]
1903-1913 [796]

LONDON CHATHAM & DOVER *[Rail 415]*
1863-1902 [111]

**MANCHESTER, SHEFFIELD &
 LINCOLNSHIRE** *[Rail 463]*
1866 *S.S.Bradford* [details delivered to
 Shipping Master at Grimsby] [250]

MIDLAND *[Rail 491]*
1904-1913 [1078]

NORTH EASTERN *[Rail 527]*
1893-1913 Accounts of voyages, list of
 crews of vessels operating at West
 Hartlepool Dock [2244]

SOUTH EASTERN *[Rail 635]*
1861-1899 [310]

**SOUTH EASTERN & CHATHAM RLY CO'S
 MANAGING COMMITTEE** *[Rail 633]*
1899-1904 [380]
1905-1909 [381]
1910-1913 [382]

STOCKTON and DARLINGTON *[Rail 667]*
1838-1839 Details of ships at Stockton
 with masters' names etc [1557]
1845-1850 Clarence staithes, Stockton,
 details of ships, masters, etc.,[1556]

YORK and NORTH MIDLAND *[Rail 770]*
1848 Crew of *ENDEAVOUR* at Selby [80]

(b) Associated company ships

These are lodged at the Public Record Office and indexed under Miscellaneous Papers and Records, *Rail 1057.* Ports of registry are given in round brackets after ships' names. Piece numbers are in square brackets.

1860-1861 Log books, agreements, release documents and accounts of crew of the foreign-going ship *RAILWAY* (London) [3556]

1861-1862 **Goole Steam Shipping Coy:** log books and accounts of voyages and crews of *S.S. COLLETIS* (London) [3563]

1862 **North Lancashire Steam Navigation Coy:** half yearly accounts of voyages and crews of *P.S. ROYAL CONSORT* (Fleetwood) between Fleetwood and Belfast [3565]

1863 **Weymouth and Channel Islands Steam Packet Coy:** half yearly accounts of voyages and crews of *P.S. CYGNUS* (Weymouth) [3568]

1865-1866 **Barrow Steam Navigation Coy*:** half-yearly accounts of voyages and crew of *P.S. ROE* (Glasgow and Lancaster) between Glasgow and Belfast and Morecambe and Belfast [3557]
(* taken over by Midland Railway Company in 1907)

1878-1880 **Port of Portsmouth and Ryde United Steam Packet Co. Ltd** (later Joint London & South Western and London, Brighton & South Coast Railway Companies): half yearly agreements and accounts of voyages of *P.S. ALBERT EDWARD* (Portsmouth) [3566]

1893-1901 **Isle of Wight Steam Packet Coy:** various log books and half-yearly agreements and accounts of voyages and crews of the home-trading ships *PRINCE OF WALES, SOUTHAMPTON, SOLENT QUEEN, HER MAJESTY, PRINCESS HELENA, PRINCESS BEATRICE, PRINCE LEOPOLD, CARISBROOKE, VECTIS, DUCHESS OF YORK* and *BALMORAL* (Southampton) [3561]

1896-1899 **Sir John Jackson's Ltd :** special half yearly accounts of voyages and crews of the home-trading [sailing] ships *PERSEVERANCE, EXPERIMENT, FOX, HARE, LILLIE, ROSIE, BEAR, TURTLE, CATHARINA, MYRTLE* and *BADGER* (Dover and London) [3564]

1897 **Galway Bay Steamboat Coy Ltd :** log books and special half yearly accounts of voyages and crews of the home-trading ships *DURAS* and *CITIE OF THE TRIBES* (Galway) [3562]

1897-1898 **Belfast Steam Navigation Coy*:** half-yearly agreements and 1903 accounts of voyages and crews of the home-trading ships: *LONDONDERRY, DONEGAL, CITY OF BELFAST, MANX QUEEN* and *DUCHESS OF DEVONSHIRE* (Barrow) [3558]
(*taken over by Midland Railway Company in 1907)

1897-1898 **City of Dublin Steam Packet Coy :** half-yearly accounts of voyages and crews of the home-trading ships *ULSTER, LEINSTER, MUNSTER, IRELAND, CONNAUGHT, KERRY, CARLOW, WICKLOW, LOUTH, GALWAY, MEATH, MAYO* and *LEITRIM* (Dublin) [3560]

1904 **River Dart Steamboat Coy :** special half-yearly accounts of voyages and crews of the home-trading ships *BERRY CASTLE, DARTMOUTH CASTLE, TOTNES CASTLE and KINGSWEAR CASTLE* (Dartmouth) [3567]

1907 **(June) Belfast Steamship Co.Ltd :** half-yearly agreement and account of voyages and crew of *S.S.GRAPHIC* (Belfast) [3559]

U.K. RAILWAY TRADE UNION RECORDS

ABBREVIATIONS:
ASEMMSMPM Amalgamated Society of Engineers, Machinists, Millwrights, Smiths and Pattern Makers
ASLEF Associated Society of Locomotive Engineers & Firemen
ASRS Associated Society of Railway Servants
NUR National Union of Railwaymen
[Formed in 1913 by amalgamation of Amalgamated Society of Railway Servants (1872), United Pointsmen's and Signalmen's Society (1880) and General Railway Workers' Union (1890)]
RCA Railway Clerks Association
TSSA Transport Salaried Staff Association
[Founded as the National Association of General Railway Clerks in 1897, later the Railway Clerks Association, then to present title in 1950.]

ABERDEEN UNIVERSITY LIBRARY
ASLEF Journal 1891-1895 and 1897-1911
NUR "Particulars of eyesight test, regulations respecting resumption of duty after sickness, holidays etc. Area promotion scheme 1925". This publication includes a complete list of names and seniority dates of footplate staff and cleaners in the L.M.S. promotion area No.2 [Old Caledonian, Old Highland and Old Glasgow & South Western - covers roughly the central area of Scotland, and south from Edinburgh and Glasgow to Carlisle, west to Oban and Ballachulish, north to Blair Atholl and Aberdeen]. There are approximately 2,500 names on the list.

BIRMINGHAM REFERENCE LIBRARY
NUR Railway Review 1971-March 1976   [SocS.BF331.8812113]
NUR Transport Review March 1976 onwards [ditto   ]
TSSA Railway Service Journal 1927-1938 [ditto   ]

DERBYSHIRE RECORD OFFICE
NUR Rowsley Branch: minutes 1916-1964 also other papers, 20th Cent. [D771]

DONCASTER LIBRARIES
RCA Doncaster Branch register of members 1916-1918 [DS 27]

GLAMORGAN ARCHIVES SERVICE
NUR Pontypridd Branch records:
    1910-1963 minute books   )
    1912-1926 balance sheets) [D/D-NUR/1]
    1913-1933 correspondence)

MANCHESTER CENTRAL LIBRARY
RCA Railway Service Journal 1932-1938, 1942-1944 [625-R9]

NOTTINGHAMSHIRE ARCHIVES OFFICE
ASRS Retford Branch minutes 1919-1949 [DD 648]

PUBLIC RECORD OFFICE, LONDON [Z/PER]
NUR The Railway Review 1907-1937 [36]
TSSA The Railway Clerk 1904-1919 [106]
TSSA Railway Service Journal 1920-1948 [106]

PUBLIC RECORD OFFICE, LONDON [Rail 1057]

ASRS:

    1875 Certificate William Keeble's membership, Clapham Jcn Branch [3393]

    1906 Certificate J.W. Keeble's membership, Paddington Branch [3394]

    c1910 Photo Reading Branch members under the Branch banner [3395]

NUR 1916 William Keeble, Clapham Jcn Branch, Disablement Fund grant [3396]

ASSEMMSPM 1835 Certificate, admission of John Chapman as member London Branch [3625]

UNIVERSITY OF WARWICK LIBRARY, [MODERN RECORDS CENTRE], COVENTRY

NUR [MSS 127] :

    Membership records 1897-1919, 1925-1927

    Volume of 1875 Branch balance sheets listing by name all members of each Branch. Later volumes detail transfers in and out with occasional lists of members of individual Branches.

    Branch minutes and registers:

        Brighton 1901, 1905-1908

        Camborne 1912-1925

        Cirencester 1899-1918

        Hornsey & Wood Green 1905-1917 (part), 1917-1919

        Stratford No.1 1926

        Wadebridge 1940's

        Walthamstow 1897-1905

        Weymouth 1912-1924

    NUR Journals:

        Railway Express 1890-1892, Railway Review from 1882

ASLEF [Included in NUR files MSS 127]

    Locomotive journal 1921-1925, 1927-1933

TSSA [MSS 55]

    Branch minutes and registers:

        Accrington 1944-1964

        Huddersfield 1900-1917

        Lincoln 1920-1961, 1916-1961

        Liverpool Street 1915-1921

        London North West 1908-1914, 1917-1919

        Middlesborough No.1 1907-1953

        Nottingham 1897-1900, 1898-1903

        Sheffield 1900-1907

        Walsall 1918-1973

        Wisbech 1908-1919, 1933-1955, 1908-1956

    TSSA Journals:

        Railway Herald 1896-1899

        Railway Clerk/Railway Service Journal 1904, 1908-1923

WARWICK & LEAMINGTON LABOUR PARTY [MSS 133]

Tapes and transcripts of interviews with V. Crumpton and Reuben Wright. Both were railwaymen and the interviews include biographical information.

Aberdeen City Libraries
Great North Review, the journal of the
    Great North of Scotland Railway
    Association from 1964. Includes items
    on some of the railway staff

Aberdeen University Library
Great North Review from 1964
GWR Mag 1905-1916
L&NER Mag 1941-1947
Railway Gazette 1945, Dec 1948-Feb
    1951

Barrow Library
(Fred Barnes Collection)
Furness Railway Mag 1897-1899
    [LC 2QA/RA1]
Furness Railway Mag 1921-1923
    [LC 100QA/FUR]
LMSR Mag 1923-1927
    [LC 2QA/LON]

Birmingham Reference Library [SocS]
BR LM Region Mag, 1950-1963
    [B384.10942]
BR Western Region Mag, 1948-1963
    [B385.10942]
Directory of Railway Officials and
    Yearbook, 1950-1951,1966-71
    [B385.1]
GWR Mag 1888-1947 [B385.10942]
L&NER Mag 1927-1939 [B385.10942]
LM&SR Mag Nov 1923-1939.
    [B385.10942]
Railway and Travel Monthly, May 1910-
    Dec 1918 [B385]
Railway Diary and Officials Directory,1918
    [B385.1]
Universal Directory of Railway Officials
    and Yearbook, 1922-1949/50
    [B385.1]
Railway Gazette, 1916-1971 (gaps)
    [BQ656.05]
Railway Gazette International, from 1972
    [B656.05]
Railway Magazine, from 1897
    [B385.10942]
Railway Times, 1838-39, 1846, 1856
    [B385.10942]
Railway Yearbook, 1902-1932 [B385]

Bishopsgate Institute, London
The Institute specialises in the London area
    and holdings of railway material
    amount to many hundreds of items.
    It also has extensive holdings of British
    Rail Union material and a wide range
    of printed books and pamphlets.

Bristol Reference Library
BR Western Region Mag, 1948-Sept 1949
GWR Mag 1891-1947 (some gaps)

Brunel University Library
BR (Southern Region) Mag 1948-1949
GER Mag 1911-1919
GWR Mag 1888-1890 1904-1947
LM&S Mag 1930-1935
L&NER Mag 1927-1943, 1945-1947
NER Mag 1911-1921, 1923
NE & Scottish (LNER) Mag 1924-1926
S.R. Mag 1923, 1928-1933, 1936-
    1937,1940-1947

Darlington Railway Centre
BR (Eastern Region) Mag 1950-June 1963
BR (Eastern, North Eastern & Scottish
    Region) Mag 1948-1949
BR (North Eastern Region) Mag 1950-
    1963 (with gaps)
L&NER Mag 1927 (part), 1930 (part),
    1944, 1946 (part), 1947
L&NER, NE & Scottish Mag Dec 1924,
    Feb 1925
NER Mag 1911--1923 (with gaps)
Rail News June 19673-1988, Jan 1989,
    1991 to date
Railway Magazine Sept 1899, Jan-June
    1923,Sept 1959, Nov 1964, Feb-Dec
    1965,1966-1969, Jan,Feb,Mar 1970,
    Mar,June, July, Aug 1972,June-Dec
    1973, 1974-Oct 1994.

Doncaster Central Library
Railway Gazette 1951-1984, June 1988
    to date
Railway Herald 1895
Railway Mag Jan-June 1910, July-Dec
    1928, July-Dec 1938. 1951. 1955
    (vol 101) to date.

Great Western Trust, Didcot
BR (W Region) Mag 1948-1962 (some
    months wanting)
GWR Mag 1891-1894, 1897-1898,1901-
    1903,1905-1907

Hampshire Record Office
BR Southern Region Mag 1951-1953
    [72M94/4/1-34]

Kent County Library
Railnews from 1980

Leicester University Library
A wide range of staff magazines and
    periodicals. Not listed.

Manchester Central Library
GCR Mag 1905-1917 [625.05.G1]
GWR Mag 1922-1939 [625.05.G5]
L&NER Mag 1933-1947 [625.05.L1]

Mitchell Library, Glasgow
A wide range of periodicals and directories
    which may contain useful information,
    especially for Glasgow.

National Railway Museum, York
BR Magazines post-1948
Furness Railway Mag 1921-1923
GCR Journal 1905-1918
GER Mag 1911-1926
GWR Mag 1892-1947
L&NER Mag 1927-1947
L&NWR Gazette 1915,.1917
LM&SR Mag 1923-1939
NER Mag 1911-1923
NE&Scottish R Mag 1924-1926
South Western Gazette 1881-1883
South Western Railway Mag 1922
Southern Railway Mag 1923-1947

Newton Abbot Library
GWR Magazine 1908-1947
Railway Magazine From 1897

Nottinghamshire Archive Office
The Railway Intelligence No.7 1853 [DDH
    55/51]

Public Record Office, London [ZPER]
BR(E Region) Mag 1950-June 1963 [21]
BR(E,NE & Scottish Regions) Mag 1948-
    1949 [17]
BR(LM Region) Mag 1950-June 1963 [22]
BR(NE Region) Mag 1950-June 1963 [25]
BR(Scottish Region) Mag 1950-June 1963
    [23]
BR(Southern Region) Mag 1950-June
    1963 [24]
BR(W Region) Mag 1950-June 1963 [20]
BT Docks Mag 1964-1981 (few months
    wanting) [114]
BT Police Journal 1950-1980 (two issues
    wanting) [61]
GCR Mag 1905-1918 [18]
GER Mag 1911-1926 [16]
GWR Mag 1862-1864 [85]
GWR Mag 1888-1949 [19]
GWR Secretary's Office Mag 1871-1880
    [44]
GWR Athletic News Nov 1905-June 1906
    [44]
GWR Paddington Goods Station staff Mag
    'The Josser'. Issues 1,2,5.No dates.
LM&SR Mag 1923-1938 [14]
LM&SR "On Time" 1934-1939 [15]
LM&SR "Quota" 1938-1939 [15]
LM&SR "Carry On" 1939-1949 [15]
L&NER Mag 1924-1947 [17]
L&NER Wartime HQ Staff Bulletin
    "Ballyhoo Review" 1939-1940 [132]
L&NWR Gazette 1914-1923 [13]
London Railways Athletic Assoc Year Book
    1913-1922 [84]
North Eastern Express (North Eastern
    Railway Association journal) 1961-
    1971 [88]
North Eastern News 1960-1962, Feb
    1963 [91]
NER Mag 1911-1923 [63]
Rail News 1971-1980 (gaps) [98]
Rail News (E Region) 1963-1970 [103]
Rail News (LM Region) 1963-1970 [98]
Rail News (NE Region) 1963-1967 [99]
Rail News (Sc Region) 1963-1970 [100]
Rail News (S Region) 1963-1970 [101]
Rail News (W Region) 1963-1970 [102]
Railway Athletic Assoc Year Book 1927-
    1939 [84]
Railway Police Journal 1949 [61]
South Western Gazette 1881-1915 [11]
South Western Mag 1916-1922 [11]

Public Record Office, London (Cont)
Southern Railway Mag 1923-1949 [12]
Southern Railway Home Guard news
 review1941-1945 [96]

Scottish Record Office
BR Mag (Scottish Region) 1948-1963
BT Staff News (Scottish) 1950-1954
 (gaps)
Edinburgh Div Bulletin (BRSc Region) 1965
LM&SR Mag 1923-1936,1938-1939
L&NER Mag 1927-1947
NER Mag 1911-1922
NE & Sc (LNER) Magazine 1923-1926
Rail News + Railnews 1963 to date

Somerset County Reference Library
GWR Mag 1905-1924

Swindon Divisional Reference Library
GWR Mag 1888-1894, 1903-1947

Widnes Library
Railway Gazette 1922-1928,
 1949 to date
Railway Mag, 1897 to date
The Library also holds an extensive
 collection of books and journals
 relating to railways.

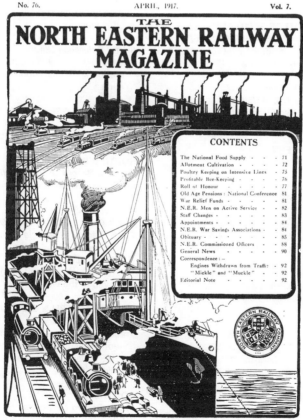

No. 76.   APRIL, 1917.   Vol. 7.

THE NORTH EASTERN RAILWAY MAGAZINE

CONTENTS

PRICE ONE PENNY.

RAILWAY STAFF AND WAR SERVICE

Companies produced a "Roll of Honour" for the 1914-18 war, listing staff in their various departments who lost their lives. These were framed, and some are still to be seen at stations throughout the UK. Stations and offices at which Rolls of Honour exist are not listed because their locations are subject to changes when reorganisations, reconstruction or development takes place. Many stations had war memorials like that on platform 1 at Paddington, at which Remembrance Services attended by General Managers have been held annually on Armistice Day.

The staff magazines covering the years of the first and second world wars contain considerable material relating to staff in the Forces, including lists of those killed or wounded, letters and photographs from men and women overseas, awards for gallantry, and entertainment and hospitality by Red Cross workers at stations and offices. In the years following the first world war the *Railway Magazine* also carried information regarding staff of individual companies who served in HM Forces.

GREAT EASTERN
Public Record Office [Rail 227]
1942-1946 Various staff records including those joining and returning after military service [542]
This register closed for 50 years

GREAT NORTH OF SCOTLAND
Scottish Record Office [BR/GNS/15]
ND Photo of memorial tablet to staff who died in world war 1. [30]

GREAT NORTHERN
Public Record Office [Rail 236]
1886-1920 Reg Supt's Office clerks including Army Reserve list [745]

GREAT WESTERN
Public Record Office [Rail 253]
1915-1918 Letters from Paddington Audit Office staff in HM Forces, with photos [516]

Public Record Office [Rail 258]
1933-1947 'Old Contemptibles' and 1914/15 Star GWR Assn [486]

Public Record Office [Rail 1014]
1900 Photo, GWR Infantry Coy, 2nd South Middlesex Volunteers [37/7/2]

LANCASHIRE & YORKSHIRE
Public Record Office [Rail 343]
1915 Roll of Honour for staff who joined HM Forces 1914-1915 [755]

LONDON BRIGHTON & SOUTH COAST
Public Record Office [Rail 414]
1914-1920 Staff of all departments on active service [791] Index [792]

MIDLAND
Bedfordshire Record Office [X 770/6]
1921 Printed memorial book for staff killed in the 1914-1918 war. Contains names, rank and unit, also position, department and station on the railway. Also list of decorations conferred on employees.

Bristol Reference Library
1914-1919 Roll of Honour, Bristol Goods station staff, first world war. 206 names.

Public Record Office [Rail 491]
1914-1918 Photo, staff of Estate Agent, Derby, in HM Forces [1065]

NORTH BRITISH
Scottish Record Office [BR/NBR/15]
1919 Staff killed in world war 1. [200]

NORTH EASTERN
Public Record Office [Rail 527]
1916 Tempy female clerical appt's with summaries of staff from CME's Dept in HM Service [1926]
1917-1930 Histories of staff who served in the war [1950]

SOUTH EASTERN & CHATHAM
Kent County Library
Three Rolls of Honour for staff killed in world war 1. CME's Dept Ashford; CME's Dept (general) and one dept unidentified

SOUTHERN
Public Record Office [Rail 651]
1939-1945 Staff decisions during Second World War [3]

RAILWAY POLICE RECORDS

This section lists railway police records which are available for public inspection. British Transport Police hold limited records which require processing. In the meantime the Chief Constable has kindly agreed that efforts will be made to assist with enquiries addressed to British Transport Police, Personnel Department, PO Box 260, 15 Tavistock Place, London WC1H 9SJ.

ASHBY AND NUNEATON JUNCTION
Public Record Office [Rail 410]
1902-1910 Traffic, police and telegraph depts of L&NW and A&NJ [1801]

BIRMINGHAM AND OXFORD JUNCTION
Public Record Office [Rail 39]
1852-1853 Guard book of accountants vouchers with details of policemens wages [15]

CORNWALL
Public Record Office [Rail 134]
1.11.1871 Memorial from inhabitants of St. Austell protesting against dismissal of W.Tucker, railway policeman and luggage attendant [62]

EAST LINCOLNSHIRE JOINT COMMITTEE
Public Record Office [Rail 177]
1848-1850 Pay list various staff including police [21]

GREAT WESTERN
Devon Record Office
1873-1874 George Stuart, policeman, service certificate [588M/F5]

Public Record Office [Rail 258]
1923-1930; 1945-1946 Chief of Police: annual reports : establishment of residential police training school [347]

Public Record Office [Rail 264]
1839-1877 Reg booking constables etc [414]

Public Record Office [Rail 1014]
1837 and 1846 Swearing in of Special Constables [3/35/1]
1839 Letter from Chief Insp of GWR Police to Editor of "The Times" vindicating his conduct in "locking up" a child of 10 years for picking flowers on the slopes at Paddington Station more familiarly known as "The Lawn" [4/47]
1839 and 1842 Recommendation for appt as police officer [3/35/2]

GREAT WESTERN (Continued)
Public Record Office [Rail 1014] (Cont)
1853 and 1854 Form of enrolment for policemen and others with letter re Directors policy re wage increases [31]
1856 Form giving details of constables duty - police dept at Malvern Wells signal box [31]

HULL AND BARNSLEY
Public Record Office [Rail 312]
1911 Alexandra Dock, appointment of special constables [130]

LEEDS AND YORK
Public Record Office [Rail 1006]
N.D. First railway policeman [80]

LEEDS NORTHERN
Public Record Office [Rail 357]
1847-1849 Police officers' time books [39 + 40]

LONDON AND NORTH EASTERN
Public Record Office [Rail 390]
1923-1947 Police annual reports [1584]

LONDON & NORTH WESTERN AND MIDLAND JOINT COMMITTEE
Public Record Office [Rail 406]
1861-1911 Staff reg of coaching and police depts at Birmingham New Street and Derby stations [16]

LONDON AND NORTH WESTERN
Public Record Office [Rail 410]
1845-1847 London & Bgham and L&NW coaching and police committee[141]
1847-1850   ditto [142]
-    Index to minutes of coaching and police committee [143]
1850-1889 Staff records, coaching, traffic and police   [1797]
1853-1876   ditto [1798]
1867-1901   ditto [1799]
1861-1912 Old Northampton staff reg, coaching and police dept [1814]
1878-1912   ditto [1815]

LONDON AND NORTH WESTERN RAILWAY (Cont)
Public Record Office [Rail 410] (Cont)
1862 Appln for post as policeman. Disqualification as over 30 years of age [1567/4]

1872-1907 Discipline book [1832]

1900-1915 Discipline book [1833]

1875-1911 Coaching and police depts [1802]

1894-1910 Coaching, police and traffic etc depts [1803 + 1804]

1902-1910 Traffic, police and telegraph depts of L&NW and Ashby & Nuneaton Jcn [1801]

LONDON AND SOUTHAMPTON
Public Record Office [Rail 412]
1839-1845 Departmental committees including police [3 + 4]

LONDON MIDLAND & SCOTTISH
Public Record Office (Rail 1015)
1845 Liverpool Central Police Office - two notices of goods stolen or taken by mistake - reward offered [2]

MIDDLESBOROUGH AND REDCAR
Public Record Office [Rail 484]
1845-1847 Police monthly paybills, with accounts for staves, lanterns and handcuffs [41]

1846-1847 Police appln for season ticket and other subjects [28]

NORTH EASTERN
Public Record Office [Rail 527]
1910 Police organisation, reports and comparisons with police forces of other companies, duties and rates of pay [1036]

1914 Hull Joint Dock, appointment of special constables [2255]

NORTH LONDON
Public Record Office [Rail 529]
1906 Staff reg coaching and police [131]

SOUTH DEVON
Public Record Office [Rail 631]
1860 Time book, W. Pike, policeman Torre [62]

SOUTH DURHAM AND LANCASHIRE UNION
Public Record Office [Rail 632]
1858 Chief Constable of Westmoreland's proposal to take command of a railway constable, with details of duties, pay and uniform [54]

STOCKTON AND DARLINGTON
Public Record Office [Rail 667]
1826-1840 Police regulations on the railways with details of accidents [485]

1833-1865 Guidance of police officers 1842 among other matters [633]

1840 Appln from Robert Swinburne, police officer of Middlesborough, asking for permission to travel on the company's coaches without payment when in performance of his duties [790]

1840-1845 Accounts for supply of police uniforms and equipment [1587]

1840-1847 Monthly pay, police officers, gatekeepers, watchmen [1307]

1846-1849 Letters from Thos Manton, Chief of Police, re accidents and all forms of adverse working, inc one re George Watkinson transported for 14 years for breaking open a cabin and stealing a coat [1248]

1865 Police and gatekeepers' salaries [1499]

TAFF VALE
Public Record Office [Rail 684]
1857-1858 Boots for police and others [55]

1858 Summer clothing for policemen, together with list of policemen giving name, number and station [55]

1858 Winter clothing for policemen [55]

1873 Police lodges at Ynyshir and Pontypridd [55]

ARCHIVISTS' HISTORICAL MISCELLANEA
Public Record Office [Rail 1005]
- Railway police; including original corres [107]

ARCHIVISTS' HISTORICAL MISCELLANEA (YORK COLLECTION)
Public Record Office [Rail 1006]
1957-1965 Leeds & York Rly, the first railway policeman [80]
1959 Article by Wm. O. Gay M.A. in Police Journal [17]

REPORTS OF COMMITTEES
Public Record Office [Rail 1124]
1919 Police Services: reports

MISCELLANEOUS PAPERS AND RECORDS
Public Record Office [Rail 1057]
1859 Copy of bye-laws, rules etc with paper seal and stamped 'Supt of Police' [1713]
1889-1890 Prosecution by J.O'Gorman, Bute Docks Police (Cardiff) of Alfred Sweet and others for fouling points on a railway at Bute Dock [1342]

RULE BOOKS ETC.
Public Record Office [Rail 1134]
1876 Police dept [414]
1906 Rule books: police (GWR) [173]
1914 Police Superannuation Society [415]
1915 Rule books: special police (GWR) [180]
1921 Rule books: police (GWR) [174]
1928 Police manual (LNER) [235]
1928 Police manual (LMSR) [322]
1934 Rule books: police (GWR) [175]
1942 Police manual (SR) [508]
ND Rule books: special police (GWR) [181]

Public Record Office [Rail 1135]
1906 Guidance to Railway officials re police regulations [55]
1920 Railway police manual (Executive Cttee) [479]

RAILWAY STAFF CONFERENCE CORRESPONDENCE AND PAPERS
Public Record Office [Rail 1172]
1919-1921 Railway police correspondence [1186]
1919-1922 Corres, inc wage scales GER Jan 1914 [1187]
1920-1922 ditto, includes copy of form of oath given by special constables LB&SCR and of special constable's warrant card NBR [1188]
1922-1924 Correspondence [1189]

RAILWAY STAFF CONFERENCE (Cont)
Public Record Office [Rail 1172] (Cont)
1923-1924 Corres, inc agreement re rates of pay and conditions of service 1920 [1190]
1925-1938 Correspondence [1191]
1919-1921 Federations scheme, witnesses in disciplinary charges [1192]
1922-1936 ditto [1193]
1941-1946 Representation of special constables on police line conference [1194]
1921-1928 Cost of living bonus [1195]
1920-1921 Supervisory staff [1196]
1920 Overtime and Sunday duty [1197]
1922 Clothing allowance when absent through sickness [1198]
1920-1921 Metropolitan [1200]
1922-1923 Dismissal of Inspector Luck GNR [1201]

WAR OF 1939-1945: RAILWAY EXECUTIVE COMMITTEE FILES
Public Record Office [AN2]
These files cover many aspects of the work of railway police. The following are some which have a genealogical interest.
Recruitment of volunteers, including special constables [1]
Police Constable E.Hall. Application for deferment [304]
Adams S.C. schedule of reserved occupations - railway police [427]
Award for gallantry. Detective Sergeant William Parker Huddart, LMS Police Officer [532]
Railway police - post-war credits [575]
Issue of passes to certain senior police officers of the Metropolitan Police [584]
Indemnities - railway police staff working on behalf of the Admiralty [604]

PHOTOGRAPHS AND PORTRAITS

Unless otherwise stated, references are to photographs. In addition to the items listed here, many photographs of individuals and groups appear in company staff magazines in association with reports of retirements, deaths and social occasions. *Railway Gazette* and *Railway Magazine* also contain many photographs of individuals.

BRAMPTON JUNCTION
Cumbria Record Office
N.D.[1913] Opening of railway and staff [PR60/21/151]

CALEDONIAN
Scottish Record Office [BR/CAL/4]
1896 Loco Officers, St. Rollox [199]
19th Cen. Staff at Larbert? [263]
1900 Caledonian Railway Officers [56A + 163]

Scottish Record Office [BR/CAL/15]
N.D. Portrait, Donald Matheson, General Manager [19]

CAMBRIAN
Public Record Office [Rail 92]
1909 Oswestry Works staff [136]

GREAT EASTERN
Public Record Office [Rail 227]
1893 Chairman, General Manager and Secretary and delegates of GER Pension Fund [509]
1894 Chairman, General Manager and members of GER management, Secretary and delegates of GER Pension Fund [510]
c1899-1910 J. Gooday {Gen. Mgr.), H.G. Drury (SOL), J. Holden (Loco Supt) [376]
c1913 Liverpool Street Station Swimming Club [511]

Suffolk Record Office [SPS]
c1904 J. Smith, shunter, Snape [609]
c1904 Porter at Snape [11595]
1919 Mr. Buck, S.Master, Clare [9344]
1959 Mr. Graham, Station Master [5603]
N.D. Stowmarket station staff [8552]
N.D. Porter at Walton [9239]
N.D. Staff at Bealings [10345]
N.D. S.M. and staff, Clare [9345 + 9346]
N.D. Halesworth station and staff [112]
N.D. Ipswich shed staff on loco [5374 + 5378]

GREAT EASTERN (Cont)
Suffolk Record Office (Cont)
N.D. Porter at Needham [1617]
N.D. Porters at Needham [8169]

GREAT NORTH OF SCOTLAND
Scottish Record Office [BR/GNS/4]
N.D. Workmen Inverurie ? [43]
N.D. Staff houses Inverurie [44]

Scottish Record Office [BR/GNS/15]
1909 and 1917 Apprentices and group at Inverurie [29]
N.D. Memorial tablet to staff who died in World War One [30]
N.D. Thomas Heywood, Loco Supt. [31]

GREAT NORTHERN
Public Record Office [Rail 1014]
c1905 Doncaster staff [33/24]
c1909 Doncaster staff [33/25]

GREAT WESTERN
Public Record Office [Rail 253]
1840-1947 Portraits of Directors and Officers (with histories) [487]
c1904 GWR cricket team West of England tour [459]
1915-1918 Paddington Audit staff in HM Forces [516]

Public Record Office [Rail 1014]
1900 GWR Infantry Coy, 2nd South Middlesex Volunteers [37/7/2]
1901 Ludgershall staff [36/16]
1902 Ilminster staff [36/17]
1904 Westbourne Park staff [33/22]
c1912 Cartage staff, Mint stables, Paddington [33/23]
N.D. Swindon's first band [38/32]
N.D. Swindon Firemens group [48/31]

GREAT WESTERN RAILWAY, MECHANICS INSTITUTE, SWINDON
Public Record Office [Rail 276]
1848-1947 Photographs, among other documents relating to Swindon and North Wilts Technical School [22]

HIGHLAND
Scottish Record Office [BR/HR/15]
N.D. Staff group with Scottish Railways
Ambulance shield [4]

LANCASHIRE AND YORKSHIRE
Public Record Office [Rail 343]
1917 CME's dept female staff [725]

LANCASHIRE AND YORKSHIRE AND GREAT NORTHERN JOINT STATION COMMITTEE
Public Record Office [Rail 341]
pre-1907 Knottingley station staff [7]

LONDON AND NORTH EASTERN
Scottish Record Office [BR/LNE/15]
1923 Staff at Leith Walk [87]
N.D. Aberdeen, presentation of Safety First
awards [91]
N.D. Inverurie Works Fire Brigade [92]

Scottish Record Office
Misc Collections [GD1]
c1923 Footplate staff at St. Margarets
Edinburgh [908/9]

LONDON AND NORTH WESTERN
Bedfordshire Record Office
Photograph album [Z 587/1] inscribed
"T.G.Gillett, a gift by his fellow clerks
on leaving Watford April 20th 1874".
The following are some of the
photographs included:
c1880 Fred Gillett in L&NWR uniform.
c1865 Thomas Gillett (1815-1904,
Lidlington Stationmaster 1854-1887)
with his son Charles.
1872 Memorial card. Thomas Cooke,
accidentally killed at Watford Goods
Station July 1872, aged 42 years.
Interred Watford Cemetery, July 22.

Further photograph album including:
c1914 Scene at Bethesda station, Wales.
Stationmaster Charles E Gillett (1853-
1935),Goods clerk and lady booking
clerk on platform. [Z587/2].
C1900-1920's Albert Clark, trolleyman at
Potton [X758/1/10 (2-6)]
1958 Photo of press article re "Long
service watches to Biggleswade men (ex
LNE, formerly GN), A. Swain, C. Sale
and A. Jordan". [X758/1/2 (80)]

LONDON AND NORTH WESTERN (Cont)
Public Record Office [Rail 410]
Nine photos of Co's hostel and houses at
Willesden, built for enginemen (photos
taken March 1966) [1377]

LONDON AND SOUTH WESTERN
Hampshire Record Office
c1900's-1950's Droxford station (Meon
Valley Rly) trains, employees and
workers who built the railway
[217M84/7]

LONDON TILBURY AND SOUTHEND
Public Record Office [Rail 437]
1912 Album, including Thomas and Robert
Whitelegg, Loco Supts. [42]

MARYPORT AND CARLISLE
Public Record Office [Rail 472]
1917 Mealsgate station staff [53]

MIDLAND
Public Record Office [Rail 491]
1899 Barnsley Court House stn staff [835]
1914-1918 Staff of Estate Agent Derby in
HM Forces [1065]

MIDLAND AND SOUTH WESTERN JCN
Public Record Office [Rail 1014]
1901 Ludgershall staff [36/16]

MID-SUFFOLK LIGHT
Suffolk Record Office [SPS]
N.D. Woman porter in office, line closure
[9240]
N.D. Gatekeeper and last train [9257]

NORTH BRITISH
Scottish Record Office [BR/NBR/15]
c1900-1905 NBR Literary Society visit to
Methil Dock [210]
1903 Loco staff at Thornton [211]
1905 Edinburgh Waverley staff [212]
N.D. W.F. Jackson, General Manager [213]

NORTH STAFFORDSHIRE
Public Record Office [Rail 1057]
1912 Photo of portrait William Douglas
Phillips, Gen. Mgr.[3523]

PERSONAL ACCIDENTS, WORKMEN'S COMPENSATION ETC.

See page 74 for *Cheshire Record Office* list of records re **Earlestown Wagon Works** and **Crewe Works.**

BARRY
Public Record Office [Rail 23]
Registers of accidents
1907-1922 Passengers and staff [53]
1898-1906 Wages staff [54]
1906-1908 " " [55]
1909-1910 " " [56]
1911-1913 " " [57]

BRECON & MERTHYR TYDFIL JUNCTION
Public Record Office [Rail 65]
1912-1917 Accident book [34]
1917-1922 Accident book [35]

Public Record Office [Rail 1057]
Individual accident files:
1882 May 20 John Davies - Driver [32]
1882 Oct Frederick Smith - Wagon Examiner [44]
1882 Oct 28 Stedman - Guard [45]
1883 May James Reed - Ganger [35]
1883 July James Johnson - Labourer [36]
1883 Aug Geo. Lewis - Goods Guard [37]
1884 Sept 8 David Davies - Passenger Driver [47]
1885 Jan 17 William Edwards - Signalman, William Coston - Passenger, S.Thomas - Passenger [39]
1885 Jan-Feb Fleur-de Lis Yard - collision between passenger train and goods wagon. William Colston injured and later died. Board of Trade Enquiry [48]
1885 May 9 J. Powell - Platelayer [40]
1886 Aug William Adams - Goods Guard [42]
1887 Feb David Griffiths - Platelayer [43]
1887 Dec Mrs. Edwards - Passenger [50]
1888 Dec Robert Thorpe - Goods Guard [49]
1891 Dec-1892 Aug W.J. Grant - passenger [51]

BRITISH RAIL (LONDON MIDLAND REGION)
Cheshire Record Office
Crewe Works [NPR4459/]
1944-1952 Report book inc **LMS** [51]
1946-1959 Comp reg inc **LMS** [58]
1960-1969 Comp reg [59]

BRITISH RAIL (SCOTTISH REGION)
Scottish Record Office [BR/RSR]15]
1949-1955 Reg staff accidents [255]

CALEDONIAN
Scottish Record Office [BR/CAL/15]
1923 Casualties and offences [16]

CAMBRIAN
Public Record Office [Rail 92]
1898-1906 Staff accidents on duty [147]
1919-1922 Staff accidents on duty [148]

CARDIFF
Public Record Office [Rail 97]
1908-1914 Accidents [37]
1914-1917 " [38]
1918 " [39]
1919 " [40]
1920 " [41]
1921-1922 " [42]
1922-1923 " [43]

GREAT CENTRAL
Public Record Office [Rail 226]
1898-1904 Workmens' comp claims [386]

GREAT EASTERN
Public Record Office [Rail 227]
1903-1922 Accident book all grades [5451]

GREAT WESTERN
Public Record Office [Rail 253]
1932-1934 CME's Dept, Swindon, job applns also staff accidents [322]

Public Record Office [Rail 264]
1911 Reg staff accidents [445]
1913 Reg staff accidents [446]
1914 Reg staff accidents [447]
1916-1918 Inquiries and reports, staff accidents [448]

LANCASHIRE & YORKSHIRE
Greater Manchester County Record Office [A18]
The following records are for Horwich Works.

1898-1935 Accident registers (41 volumes) [1 - 41]
1898-1959 Accident compensation payments (21 volumes) [2/1-21]

LANCASHIRE & YORKSHIRE (Cont)
Greater Manchester County Record Office
[A18] (Cont)
Horwich Works (Cont)
1902-1908 Workmens Comp Act reg of accidents [3/1]
1924-1958 Workmens Comp Act returns (35 volumes) [3/2-36]
1922-1927 Workmens Comp Act non-claims (6 volumes) [3/37-42]
1884 Particulars of accidents [3/43]
1893-1948 Particulars of workmen wearing surgical appliances [3/44]
1918-1919 Medical examinations [3/45]
1928,1947 Instructions and circulars [3/46]
1937-1940 Investigations [3/47]
1950-1964 Returns of compensation and ex-gratia payments [3/48]
1954-1971 Payments for disablement [3/49]
N.D. List of persons paid lump sums,and who are not to be employed again [3/50]
ND Accident corres. Seven boxes by surname (A-B, C-F, F-H, H-L, M-P,R-T, U-Z) [4/1-7]
1925-1941 Accident book [4/8]
1942-1960 Accident book [4/9]
1919-1925 Accident compensation cases, outdoor machinery dept. (3 volumes) [4/10-12]
1927-1932 Factory and workshop accident quarterly reports [4/13]
1949-1959 Works accident returns [4/14]
N.D. Safety in factories test reports [4/15-17]

LONDON AND BIRMINGHAM
Public Record Office [Rail 384]
1835 Watford tunnel accident. Report with names of men killed [261]

LONDON AND NORTH EASTERN
Scottish Record Office [BR/LNE/15]
1925-1937 Staff accidents reports and corres, discipline offences [57-68]

LONDON AND NORTH WESTERN
Cheshire Record Office
1907-1923 Crewe Works Comp regs [NPR4459/52-55]

LONDON AND NORTH WESTERN (Cont)
Public Record Office [Rail 410]
June 1969 Returns of accident pay [1986]

LONDON AND SOUTH WESTERN
Hampshire Record Office [67M90]
1912-1923 Workmen's Comp Act payments (part of 8 volumes unlisted)
1924 As above, includes **Southern Railway**

LONDON BRIGHTON AND SOUTH COAST
Public Record Office [Rail 414]
1889-1904 Workmens comp returns [750]
1892-1898 Workmen's comp claimants Brighton Works [756]
1899-1902 Workmen's comp claimants Brighton Works [757]
1911 Workmens compensation cases [873]

LONDON CHATHAM AND DOVER
Public Record Office [Rail 415]
1880-1891 Injuries to workmen [108]

LONDON MIDLAND & SCOTTISH
Cheshire Record Office
Crewe Works [NPR 4459/]
1924-1945 Comp regs [56-57]
1946-1959 Comp regs (inc **BRLMR**) [58]

Outdoor Department
1937-1948 Report book [47]

C.M.E.'s Department
1934-1944 Report books [48-50]
1944-1952 Report books (inc **BRLMR**) [43-46]

MARYPORT AND CARLISLE
Public Record Office [Rail 472]
1861-1912 Accidents and offences, drivers and firemen [51]

MIDLAND
Public Record Office [Rail 491]

1875-1888 Accidents, staff and others		[1058]
1888-1895	ditto	[1059]
1895-1901	ditto	[1060]
1901-1906	ditto	[1061]
1914-1921	ditto	[1062]

MIDLAND (Cont)
Public Record Office [Rail 491] (Cont)
1908 Workmens comp cases
		[1042 + 1043]
1909	ditto	[1044 + 1045]
1910	ditto	[1046 + 1047]
1911	ditto	[1048 + 1049]
1912	ditto	[1050 + 1051]
1913	ditto	[1052 + 1053]
1914	ditto	[1054 + 1055]
1915	ditto	[1056 + 1057]

NORTH BRITISH
Scottish Record Office [BR/NBR/15]
1903-1906 Workmens comp claims [197]

NORTH EASTERN
Public Record Office [Rail 527]
1881-1882 Injury to an engineman [1904]
1912 Claim by a clerk involved in an
accident off duty [1922]

RHYMNEY
Public Record Office [Rail 583]
1896-1922 Accidents and superannuation
allowances LC&W Dept. [61]
1907-1922 Staff accidents reported to
Inspector of Factories LC&W Dept [62]
1908-1913 Staff accidents reported to
Board of Trade [63]
1913-1919 Staff accidents reported to
Board of Trade [64]
1920-1922 Staff accidents reported to
Board of Trade [65]

SOUTH EASTERN AND CHATHAM RAILWAY COMPANY'S MANAGING COMMITTEE
Public Record Office [Rail 633]
1912 Minor accidents 1st quarter [440]

SOUTHERN
Dorset Record Office
1943 Death certificate, Fred Stroud, killed
by locomotive Sherborne [D720/2]

Hampshire Record Office [67M90]
1944-1945 Workmen's Comp Act
payments (part of 8 volumes, unlisted)

Public Record Office [Rail 651]
1927-1957 Workmens comp cases,
Brighton Works [4]

STOCKTON AND DARLINGTON
Public Record Office [Rail 667]
1824-1830 Accounts for medical services
to workmen etc. [1326]
1825-1845 Thos Manton, Police Supt.,
reports re personal accidents [1209]
1831 Appln for comp for injury [1028]
1832 Memorial to Directors from staff re
death of a colleague [830]
1837-1849 Letters re personal accidents
[1246]
1854 Draft proposals for an employees
accident and sickness insurance fund
[530]

TAFF VALE
Public Record Office [Rail 258]
1922-1947 Employees Accident Fund
papers [532]

Public Record Office [Rail 684]
1897-1905 Staff accidents	[116]
1910-1914 ditto	[117]
1911-1919 ditto	[118]
1919-1922 ditto	[119]

1916-1921 Staff accidents, Board of Trade
returns [120]

Welsh Industrial and Maritime Museum
1896-1969 Employees Accident Fund
records with notes on the history of the
Fund by Mr.K.D. Lindsay, the last
Secretary,

ENTRY FOR *CHESHIRE RECORD OFFICE*
An extensive collection of accident and
compensation records is held for
Earlestown Wagon Works and **Crewe
Works.** These include records for **LNW,
LMS** and **BRLMR staff.** To split them
into the separate companies would
destroy their continuity, so they are
given here as listed by Cheshire Record
Office.
All are listed under class NPR 4111.

Earlestown Wagon Works, Newton-le-Willows
Opened by LNWR 1860, closed 1964.
Summary compensation regs
Name, brief details of accident and
compensation.
LMS   1930-1936 [1]
LMS   1937-1947 [2]
BRLMR 1947-1955 [3]

Cheshire Record Office (Cont)

Weekly compensation regs
Employees and amounts of compensation
   received weekly.
LNW   1898-1913 [4]
LNW & LMS   1913-1939 [5]
LMS & BRLMR 1940-1964 [6]

Outstations weekly comp register
As above, but refers to 15 outstations.
LMS   1933-1934 [7]

Compensation averages book
Weekly payments. Indexed.
LNW   1917-1922 [8]
LNW & LMS 1922-1927 [9]
LMS   1926-1930 [10]

Claims book
Weekly list of staff claiming benefits
LMS & BRLMR 1928-1953 [12]

Register of correspondence
Index to correspondence files and some
   claims in 1 to 3 above.
LMS & BRLMR 1928-1953

Compensation yearly reports
Annual reports.
BRLMR 1949-1964 [13]

Compensation book
Abstracts of compensation paybills for
   temporary disablement allowances.
LNW, LMS and BRLMR 1898-1962 [14]

Accident registers
Names, brief details of accident, time off
   and date resumed work.
BRLMR All departments 1955-1964 [15]
BRLMR Stores and warehouse dept
   1956-1964 [16]

Accident report book
Detailed descriptions of some of the
   accidents in 15 above. Statements from
   employees and witnesses.
BRLMR 1963-1964 [17]

Cheshire Record Office (Cont)

Departmental accident and attendance
records
Each department was allocated a random
alphabetical reference, and the function of
some departments is unclear. The accident
and time books were kept together in each
department. The former give first hand
accounts of accidents and the latter are a
weekly attendance record.

ON and TZ shops.
Accident books.
LMS Metal Machine Shop 1944-45 [18]
LMS Metal Machine Shop 1945-47 [19]
LMS Sep 1945-Mar 1947 [20]
LMS Apr-Dec 1947 [21]
LMS and BRLMR Dec 1947-Apr 1949 [22]
BRLMR 1949 - 1964 [23 - 28]
BRLMR Welding Shop 1963-1964 [29]

Time books.
BRLMR 1957 - 1964 [30-34]

Inspection Department
BRLMR Accident books 1949-1964
   [35 + 36]
BRLMR Register of dangerous occurrences
   Nov.1956-Feb.1961 [37]
BRLMR Notes on classes of accidents and
   relevant codes 1956 [38]
LMSR Time book Feb-Oct 1942 [39]

Smithy and Spring Shops
Accident books
BRLMR Jun 1955-May 1962 [40]
BRLMR Oct-1958-Sep 1962 [41]
BRLMR Jun 1959-May 1964 [42]
BRLMR Oct 1962-Mar 1964 [43]

Time book 'Yard'
BRLMR Apr-1961-Jun 1964 [44]

Maintenance Department
Accident books
BRLMR Mar 1957 - Mar 1963 [45-54]

Time books
BRLMR 1960-1964 [55-57]

Sawmill
Accident books
BRLMR 1957-1963 [59-64]
BRLMR 1952-1964 [107]

Reports of inquests into fatalities can provide useful information. From the earliest days railway accidents and subsequent inquests were reported in great detail. The *Railway Chronicle* of 3rd January 1846 contained the following comment : *"We are happy to state that the accidents during the last four weeks have been so few and unimportant as to justify us in postponing our usual MONTHLY REVIEW of them"*, and the following week the comment was *" We are happy to state that no accident whatever is reported this week to have happened to any one of the thousands who have used railways"*.

The issue of 3rd January also carried a detailed report of the opening of the inquest into the death of the two men referred to on the memorial in Ely Cathedral (see page 18 and caption). According to this their names were Thomas Pickering, the driver, and Richard Hedger, the stoker. The issue of 10th January contained further details of the inquest and that of the 17th January recorded that 12 of the 15 members of the jury agreed a verdict of "Accidental death caused by the imprudent conduct of the engine-driver in going at an excessive speed ", while the other three wished to add "... and the defective construction of the engine". The majority decision, however, prevailed.

It is an interesting case as it reveals some of the views on the relative merits of Brunel's broad gauge and Stephenson's narrow gauge as well as aspects of locomotive design.

U.K. RAILWAY APPRENTICESHIP, EDUCATIONAL AND SOCIAL ACTIVITIES

BIRKENHEAD
Public Record Office [Rail 35]
1st May 1854 Apprentice indenture, Thos Tierney, 5 years engine cleaner [33]
13th July 1854 Apprentice indenture, Thos Davies, 5 years book keeper [34]
4th March 1858 Apprentice indenture, Francis Dodd, 5 years book keeper [35]

BRISTOL AND EXETER
Somerset Record Office
1862 Henry Britton, Loco dept, 6 years proficiency certificate [T/PH/br.C/1372]

BRITISH RAIL [SCOTTISH REGION]
Scottish Record Office
Misc. Collections [GD1]
1910-1972 St. Margarets (later Edinburgh and District) Railwaymens M.I.C. minutes,**includes NB** and **LNE** [908/1 + 2, 6-8]
1925-1977 St. Margarets M.I.C. lists of members, **includes LNE** [908/3 + 4]
1940-1977 Polmadie Enginemens M.I.C. minutes, **includes LMS** [905/1]

CALEDONIAN
Scottish Record Office [BR/CAL/15]
1895-1920 Special apprentices, St. Rollox [13]

GREAT CENTRAL
Public Record Office [Rail 226]
1899-1905 Competition for railway ambulance shield [401]

GREAT EASTERN
Public Record Office [Rail 227]
1905 Programme for First Annual Meat Tea and Concert of GER Printing Works Quoit Club [365]

GREAT NORTH OF SCOTLAND
Scottish Record Office [BR/GNS/4]
1866-1873 Indenture papers, Alex Gauld and George Stephen, clerks [22]

GREAT NORTHERN
Public Record Office [Rail 1057]
1874-1903 Literary Society and Dining Club papers [3104]

GREAT WESTERN
Public Record Office [Rail 252]
1864 Apprentice indenture, John Maslin, fitter, Swindon Works [13]

Public Record Office [Rail 253]
1902-1917 Musical Society: minutes [722]
1909-1929 Musical Society: specimen programmes [724]
1909-1938 Musical Society: reports and accounts [721]
1917-1950 Musical Society: minutes [723]
1930-1934 Musical Society: specimen programmes [725]
1935-1939 Musical Society: specimen programmes [726]

Public Record Ofice [Rail 257]
1888 St. John Ambulance Assn: includes list of qualified men [12]

Public Record Office [Rail 258]
1867-1927 Enginemen and Firemen's Mutual Assn: corres etc [298 + 299]
1873-1930 GWR Medical Fund Society (Swindon), papers etc [411]
1880-1931 Engineering pupils: conditions of acceptance etc [345]
1893-1910 Engineering apprentices: conditions of acceptance etc [346]
1896-1940 Social and Educational Union: annual reports etc [429]
1897-1944 Swindon Technical School: papers [398]
1904-1928 Widows and Orphans Benevolent Fund [435 + 436]
1911-1947 Office outings [409]
1922-1932 Housing of staff: Company's schemes [292]
1923-1947 Housing loans to individuals and public utility societies [498]
1924-1945 UK Railway Officers' and Servants Assn [486]
1925 Swindon Retired Workmen's Association [485]
1925-1928 Acworth Memorial Scholarship [401]
1939-1940 Staff Assn: comforts fund; photographic section; opening of Truro Institute [428]
1942; 1944 Royal Hamadryad Seamen's Hospital: papers [439]

GREAT WESTERN (Cont)
Public Record Office [Rail 264]
1864-1922 Reg LC&WD apprentices
[279-282]
1881-1885 Timebook LC&WD apprentices
[286]
1893-1931 Regs LC&WD premium
apprentices [284 + 285]
1903-1912 Reg LC&WD apprentices,
Swindon and North Wilts Tech School
[292]
1912-1922 Regs LC&WD apprentices,
Swindon and North Wilts Tech School
[293-295]
1925-1947 Reg LC&WD apprentices at
outstations [283]

Public Record Office {Rail 276]
1848-1947 Notices etc including reports
of the Swindon & North Wilts Technical
School 1892- 1906 [22]
1851-1892 Programmes of concerts etc at
the Mechanics' Institution [23]

Public Record Office [1014]
1859-1933 Formation of GWR Clerks
Dining Club - Minutes of meeting 21
Dec 1859 and 1933 Rule Book [4/14]

Public Record Office [Rail 1057]
1881 Rents of GWR houses at Swindon
[2971]

GREAT WESTERN RAILWAY
NEW SWINDON SCHOOLS
Public Record Office [Rail 278]
1873-1879 Attendance and fees paid [5}

LANCASHIRE AND YORKSHIRE
Public Record Office [Rail 343]
1891-1908 Horwich Mechanics Institute
and Technical School annual syllabuses
and class results [721]

LONDON AND NORTH EASTERN
Scottish Record Office [BR/LNE/15]
1923-1937 T.A. minutes and Education
Committee reports [44]
1924-1938 Ambulance competition
records [84]
1925-1947 Ambulance certificate lists [46]
1938-1939 T.A.'s training reports,
Scottish Area [79]

LONDON AND NORTH WESTERN
Cheshire Record Office [NPR1/]
1861-1908 Crewe Mechanics Institute.
Various papers. [24]
1896-1904 Crewe Mechanics Institute.
Papers on the Kean Prize, presented to
apprentices following exam results [25]
1911-1961 Crewe Orphanage visitors
book. Entries do not indicate names of
children visited [28]
1920-1929 Crewe Orphanage admissions
reg. Also includes Dec.1944 to Sept.
1958 and list of children in the
Orphanage in 1944. Limited information
[27]

Public Record Office [Rail 1007]
1857 Apprentice indenture for T.A.Peterkin
[609]

Public Record Office [Rail 1057]
1853-1896 Literary Society papers [3105]

LONDON AND SOUTH WESTERN
Public Record Office [Rail 1057]
1896-1898 Institute and Club papers
[3106]

LONDON BRIGHTON AND SOUTH COAST
Public Record Office [Rail 414]
1866-1876 List of apprentices [751]
1875 Nov 15 Apprentice indenture John
Geering [794]
1885 Dec 2 Apprentice indenture Percival
Gordon Gay [793]

MIDLAND
Cumbria Record Office
1899 Plan of cottages, Scotby
[S/RD/BB/3/2/31]

Derby Local Studies Library
1896) Midland Railway Enginemen and
1897) Firemens Life Assurance Fund
1899) annual banquets

Derbyshire Record Office
1875-1937 Derby Railway Orphanage
[see page 43]

Public Record Office [Rail 491]
1892-1909 Loco dept reg including pupils
[1069]

MONMOUTHSHIRE RAILWAY AND CANAL
Public Record Office [Rail 500]
1877 Petition to the Railway Board by old drivers re cost of joining GWR Mutual Assistance Society [43]

NEATH AND BRECON
Public Record Office [Rail 1057]
1904-1910 Employees Sick and Benefit Society [1498]

NORTH BRITISH
Scottish Record Office [BR/NBR/15]
1895-1923 Ambulance competition records (201-207)
1905-1928 Staff awarded Ambulance certificates [94]
1909-1915 Scottish Railways Ambulance competition records [208]

NORTH EASTERN
Cumbria Record Office (Carlisle)
1851-1960 Literary and Benevolent Institution, Carlisle, records inc monthly subscriptions by named members (DSO/119/4)

Public Record Office [Rail 527]
1840-1876 Wages books, Shildon Works apprentices [1943-45]
1866 Tyne Dock Schools; tracings of school and vicinity [2234]
1866 Tyne Dock Schools; workmen's School Committee corres. etc [2230]
1866-1867 Tyne Dock Schools; minutes of School Committee [2229]
1866-1870 Tyne Dock Schools; general corres [2231]
1899-1900 Deductions from clerks etc for Mutual Assurance Fund [2054]
1919-1924 Reports of apprentices attending day classes [1929]
N.D. Tyne Dock Schools; plan of school [2233]

Public Record Office [Rail 1057]
Shildon Mechanics Institute, various items:
Ticket for tea and meeting 14 Oct 1871
Members ticket 189.?
Ticket for entertainment for benefit of distressed French peasantry (undated) [3740]

NORTH EASTERN (Cont)
Tyne and Wear Archive Service
1908-1959 NER Servants Pension Society records [1044/90-138]
1914-1953 NER Servants Death and Endowment Society records (later NER Servants Sickness and Assurance Society) [1044/1-89]

NORTH STAFFORDSHIRE
Public Record Office [Rail 1057]
1854 Apprentice indenture William Douglas Phillips to John Scott Russell as shipbuilder and engineer [3522]

SOUTH EASTERN
Public Record Office [Rail 1057]
1880-1881 Staff serving on local and other councils [2935]

SOUTH EASTERN AND CHATHAM RAILWAY COMPANY'S MANAGING COMMITTEE
Public Record Office [Rail 633]
1874-1911 Reg Superannuation Fund entrants [367]
1903-1909 Ashford (Newtown) schools; papers and plans for lighting and ventilation schemes [339]

STOCKTON AND DARLINGTON
Public Record Office [Rail 667]
NOTE: Title of New Shildon Mechanics Institute changed in 1906 to North Eastern Railway Mechanics Institute, Shildon, and again in 1923 to London and North Eastern Railway Institute, Shildon.
1840-1848 Letters, including one from a schoolmaster dismissed from the railway school at Waskerley [1287]
1846-1850 New Shildon Mechanics Institute membership records [1278]
1849 Superannuation scheme return of employees and wives [523]
1849-1864 Waskerley School papers and other educational matters [498]
1853 Shildon, need for scripture reader: Large wages are being earned and too often as rapidly squandered. [591]
1864 Petition to Directors from Traffic dept members of Mutual Provident Society re funds [791]

AYLESBURY
RAILWAY.

FIVE
POUNDS
REWARD.

Some evil-disposed Person or Persons have lately *feloniously Stolen and carried away*, a quantity of **RAILS, STAKES,** and **MATERIALS,** belonging to the Company, for which any Offender, on Conviction, is liable to Transportation for Seven Years.

Several **STAKES** driven into the Ground for the purpose of setting out the Line of Railway, *have also been Pulled up and Removed,* by which a Penalty of Five Pounds for each Offence has been incurred, half Payable to the Informer and half to the Company.

The above Reward will be paid on Conviction, in addition to the Penalty, to any Person who will give Evidence sufficient to Convict any Offender guilty of either of the above Crimes, on application to Mr. **HATTEN** or Mr. **ACTON TINDAL,** of Aylesbury.

By Order of the Directors.

Aylesbury, August 18th, 1838.

May, Printer, Aylesbury.

Public Record Office [Rail 437]

1894-1912 London Tilbury and Southend
Railway ledgers. Railway Clearing
system, Super Fund Association
[56 + 57]

Public Record Office (Rail 1057)

1894-1896 Vale of Glamorgan Railway
entrants to RCH Superannuation Fund
Association [1020]

Public Record Office [Rail 1085]

1842-1849 Staff salary reg [71]
1869-1899 Instructions to clerks and
examiners [27]
1872 Memorial from clerks to
Committee of RCH for general revision
of salaries throughout the office, with
separate roll containing additional
signatures [70]
1873-1921 Clearing House clerical
staff: salaries, conditions of service,
rules [128]
1888-1915 Weekly wages staff reg [14]

Public Record Office [Rail 1096]

1862-1901 Numbers and grades of
staff in various departments [1]
1939-1941 General file relating to Clearing
House staff in national emergency [2]
1940-1948 File relating to advancement
for selected staff with salary details
[3}

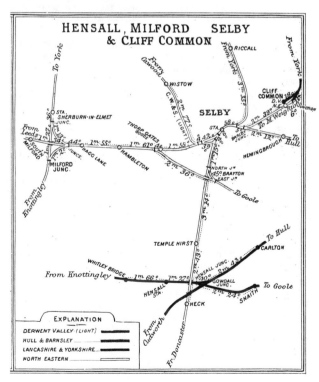

RECORDS ABROAD

EIRE

Irish Railway Record Society, Heuston Station, Dublin 8.

Contact:- Joseph Leckey, Archivist, Vestey Hall, Ballygowan BT23 6HQ. Code:- B, D, E, H

Notes:- (a) A reader's ticket is not required but the Society would expect users to join if they intend to visit the Library more than once a year.

(b) The Archivist will deal with postal enquiries at Ballygowan, but the archives are held in Dublin. Advance notice to view is desirable.

(c) Personal callers are not charged a search fee but paid research can be undertaken on behalf of enquirers.

The IRRS has brought together material known as the Irish Transport Genealogical Archive. Material is still being accessioned but it already gives access to biographies of thousands of Irish men and women employed in transport, including pre-civil registration information. A list of the I.T.G. records and other publications of the I.R.R.S. can be obtained from the publishers, The Irish Economic Press, Vestey Hall, Ballygowan, BT23 6HQ.

AUSTRALIA

J.S.Battye Library, Perth

The Library holds W.A. Govt Railways records from 1880 to c1910 covering the entire spectrum of railway workers.

A second collection is of W.A. Govt Rlys and Tramways casual employees from c1913 to the late 1940's. The collections have not yet been processed, but this is an indication of coverage:-

Traffic branch - [includes Roebourne - Cossack Tramway]. Station Master details are held by the Archive Group, Australian Historical Society [W.A. Div], GPO Box S1319, Perth, WA 6001.

Loco branch - includes loco crews, fitters, machinists etc.

Way and Works branch - gangers and track maintenance men c1890-c1905

Stores branch - 11 entries only

Head Office - 1900-1910

Early volumes based on isolated pockets - Geraldton, Bunbury, Perth.

In the early stages staff were imported from Eastern States and Britain. Many 1880's -1890's entries record details.

Australian Archives, Collinswood

Records of the following organisations and undertakings:-

Australian National Rly Commission

Australian National Rlys

Central Australian Rly

Commonwealth Rlys

Kalgoorlie - Port Augusta Rly

North Australian Rly

Port Augusta - Whyalla Rly

AUSTRALIA (Cont)

Australian Archives,Collinswood (Cont)

Port Pirie - Port Augusta Rly

Port Augusta - Government Gums Rly

Port Augusta - Oonadatta Rly

Port Augusta - Alice Springs

South Australian Rlys

State Transport Authority Board

Trans-Australian Rly

Australian Archives, Mitchell

Dept of Works and Railways records include previous Public Works Branch of the original Dept of Home Affairs. [CRS]

1902-1934 History and leave cards [A97, A172, A174, A280, CP878/9]

1911-1933 Name index cards [A151]

1912-1929 Tempy emp. cards [A264]

1912-1933 Staff corres [A197,A294,A282]

1929-1930 Reg central staff [A288]

New South Wales State Rail Authority

1870 Public Works Dept returns of employees

1871 " " "

1878 " " "

1877-1908 Dept of Railways lists of employees in the Government Gazette

From 1910 State Railway Authority staff personal history cards, held by the Finance Division. Available only to bona fide family member with written permission from employee. If deceased a 30-year closure applies.

AUSTRALIA (Cont)

**Public Record Office of South Australia
State Library, Adelaide**
South Australia Railways [GRG42/]
1853-1913 Regs indexed (some volumes
  wanting) [131]
1889-1926 Reg of appointments (mainly
  daily paid) [73]
1914-1946 Staff record, War service.
  Murray Bridge Division. Mainly World War
  Two but some World War One [177]
1956-1980 Reg of service, Murray Bridge
  Division. Details of employment of
  Australian Workers Union labourers
  (30 year restriction) [176]
- Photos of staff groups [134]

Queensland Railways Centre, Brisbane
Queensland Railways
c1865-1965 Illustrated biographies of most
  salaried officers in Chief Engineer's branch
  [PA series 70-74]
c1870-1900 "Blue books" with details of all
salaried officers [Historical collection D series]

Victoria State Transport Authority,
Victoria Railways
1884-1903 Records "ons" and "offs"
1884-1929 Records of permanent staff
1914-1918 Staff who enlisted for WW 1
  and those who died.
Also staff records with restricted access.
  Specific enquiries to the Authority.

CANADA
BC Rail, Vancouver
Details of genealogical archive sources have
  not been given, but requests will be
  dealt with in a discretionary manner.

Provincial Archives of British Columbia
The archives include extensive material
  concerning B.C. railroads, including
  papers of employees and photos.

CP Rail Corporate Archives, Montreal
Staff records have been kept since 1903.
  Only salaried staff are included as
  contractors kept their own records of
  transient workers. CP Rail will only
  consider enquiries with full name,
  approximate dates and place of work
  or position held.

CANADA (Cont)
**Ontario Northland Transportation
  Commission Archives, North Bay**
Ontario Northland Railway
1905-1986 Service history cards

Public Archives of Canada, Ottawa
Canadian Northern [RG30.Series III A.7]
1901-1911 Payrolls, general
    -        Payrolls, Western Companies
    -        Payrolls, Winnipeg terminal
1912 Employees, Winnipeg
1917 Seniority list

*Central Vermont System
  [RG30.Series III A.24]*
1933 List of employees

Grand Trunk [RG30.Series I A.8]
1862-1871 Payrolls
1889-1921 Payrolls
1886-1913 Permanent staff reg
1913-1914 Staff records,Toronto

Grand Trunk Pacific [RG30.Series I E.1]
1905-1912 Unclaimed wages records
1906-1920 Payrolls
1908-1912 Roll books

Intercolonial [RG30.Series IV A.1.g]
1891-1916 Paylists and payrolls, general
1908-1916 Payrolls, *Prince Edward Island
  Railway*

INDIA
India Office Library and Records, London
Prefix L/AG/46/ except where indicated
Bengal Central Railway
1886-1896 Staff list [4/11]

Burma Railway
1898-1921 Staff list [6/17-18]
1922-1928 Half-yearly officers list
  [L/F/10/250]

Calcutta and South East Railway
1859-1866 Staff agreements [4/13]

Covenanted railway employees
1927-1936) Annual lists
1937-1947) [L/S&G/6/64 and 860]

INDIA (Cont)
India Office Library and Records (Cont)
East Bengal Railway
1862-1869 Staff agreements [10/35]
1879-1891 Staff lists [10/35]

East India Railway
c1858-1925 Staff agreements[11/133-137]
1861-1890} Half-yearly staff lists, with ages
1911-1922}   from 1886 [11/138-141]

Great India Peninsula Railway
1881-1925 Staff agreements and index to
appointments made in U.K. 1848-1880.
[12/86-88]

Sind [Punjab, Delhi] Railway
1868-1869 Staff lists [17/12]

South Indian Railway
1891-1940 Staff agreements [18/1-4]

State Railways
1855-1946 appt's made in UK [L/F/8/1-20]
Indexes [Z/L/F/8/1-2]
1861-1904 Civil Lists, Public Works Dept
officers and workmen of State Rlys only
[V/13/195-213]
1884-1900 Staff lists [L/F/10/229-244]
1884-1953 Histories of service (staff of
privately managed railways are not
included) [V/12/51-52,54-62,66-80]
1905-1907 Civil Lists, Railways Board, Dept
and Ministry. Officers and workmen of
State railways and officers of privately
managed railways [V/13/227-243]

INDIA (Cont)
India Office Library and Records (Cont)
Lists of railway employees are given in
Bengal, Madras and Bombay
directories and in "Thacker's Indian
Directory".

The Library also holds collections of personal
papers of individuals who worked for or
had connections with Indian railways.
Many contain items of interest to family
history researchers e.g. letters, warrants
for commissions etc. These are indexed in
the European Manuscripts [Railways]
card index by name of individual.

NEW ZEALAND

New Zealand Railways, Wellington
New Zealand Government Railways and New
Zealand Railway Corporation
Service histories and some early staff files

UNITED STATES OF AMERICA

Union Pacific Railroad, Omaha
Staff records are destroyed after employees
leave the Company, but there are some
records which list officers and agents,
also staff magazines from 1921-1930
and 1960's to present day. Enquiries
must include specific information re
location.

RECORDS, INCLUDING STAFF RECORDS, FOR RAILWAYS IN SOUTH AFRICA

South Africa entered the railway age with the running of its first scheduled train in 1860 (although railway companies had been formed earlier than that), at which time it consisted of the British Colonies of the Cape of Good Hope and Natal, and the Boer republics of Orange Free State (Oranje Vri j-Staat) and Transvaal (Zuid-Afrikaansche Republiek). Medal rolls for the Anglo-Boer War (1899-1902) in connection with service in the Cape Government Railways are held by the Cape Archives Depot, and for service with the Natal Government Railways by the Natal Archives Depot.

The following are the railway companies, with their approximate dates of operation:

CAPE
1   Cape Town Railway and Dock Company 1853-72
1a Cape Town and Wellington Railway Company 18?-1872
2   Wynberg Railway Company 1861-72
3   Cape Government Railways 1873-1916
4   Cape Central Railways 1883-1892
4a New Cape Central Railways 1893-1925
5   Kowie Railway Compny 1881-?1912

TRANSVAAL
6   Nederlandsche Zuid-Afrikaansche Spoorweg-Maatschappi j (NZASM)1887-1908.
7   Lebombo Railway Company 1876-77
8   Central South African Railways 1902-10
9   Pretoria-Pietersburg Spoorwegmaatschappi j 1896-1908
10 Imperial Military Railways 1900-1902

ORANGE FREE STATE
3   Cape Government Railways 1884-96
11 Oranje Vri j-Staat Gouvernements Spoorwegen 1897-1900
8   Central South African Railways 1902-10

NATAL
12 Natal Railway Company 1860-76
13 Natal Government Railways 1875-1916

COUNTRYWIDE
14 South African Railways 1916-present, with name changes to South
    African Transport services, Spoornet (both in the 1980's).

South Africa (Continued)

ACTIVE SERVICE
15 Railways and Harbours Brigade 1921-51.
   Numerous construction and repair companies, tank workshops, as well as anti-tank units, served in the Union of South Africa as well as in East and North Africa and in Italy.

16 SARODS or South African Railways Overseas Dominions Section (World War 1)

17 Railway Regiment (short-lived, only active in German South-West Africa [Namibia] in WW1).

   For information write to one or more of the following. Appreciate that there may be some gaps and overlap and that you may have to pay a professional researcher to do most of the actual scanning of records. The numbers associated with the various organisations are those for the railways given above. Apart from one in Holland they are all in South Africa.

Nos 1 to 5
The Chief Archivist,Cape Archives Depot, Private Bag X9025 CAPE TOWN   8000.

Nos 6 to 10, also some 3, 13
The Director of Archives, Private Bag X236, PRETORIA 0001.

No 6
Algemeen Rijksarchief, DEN HAAG, Nederland (NZASM Personeelsstaaten).
   This deals with Dutch citizens who were employed by this company in the Zuid-Afrikaansche Republiek on constructing and running most of the republican Transvaal's railways up to about 1900.

Nos, 3, 11, 8, 10
The Chief Archivist, Free State Archives Depot, Private Bag X20504,
   BLOEMFONTEIN 9000.

Nos 12, 13
The Chief Archivist, Natal Archives Depot, Private Bag X9012,
   PIETERMARITZBURG   3200.

Nos 15 to 17
The Officer in Charge, Military Information Bureau, Archives Section, Private Bag X289, PRETORIA 0001

The Director, South African National Museum of Military History, PO Box
   52090, SAXONWOLD 2132.

No 14
The Curator, Spoornet Museum, PO Box 3753, JOHANNESBURG 2000.

South Africa (Continued)

RAILWAY MISSIONARY WORK

Not strictly railwaymen or women, but there were a lot of missionaries whose work was concerned solely with railway staff in the outlying areas. Try the following:

The Secretary, SAR Christian Union, PO Box 7585, JOHANNESBURG 2000.

The Archivist, Church of the Province of South Africa, Church House, Queen Victoria Street, CAPE TOWN, 8001.

Die Argivaris, Nederduits Gereformeerde Kerk, Greyspas, KAAPSTAD 8001.

I am grateful to Brian Johnson Barker of Cape Town for the information in this section.

LOCATIONS OF SOURCE MATERIAL

Research facilities at the locations are indicated by code letter, the key to which is given below:

A Reader's ticket required
B Reader's ticket not required
C Facilities are available for personal research on the premises
D Facilities are not available for personal research on the premises
E An appoitnment is essential
G An appointment is not necessary
H Postal enquiries are dealt with - in some cases limited
J Postal enquiries are not dealt with
K Search fee is charged
L Search fee is not charged
M Photocopies can be supplied
N Photocopies cannot be supplied
P Photographs of some stations can be supplied
Q Photographs cannot be supplied

Details of variables such as opening times, search fees etc., are not included here. Most locations offer leaflets giving current information and these can be obtained on application. Some locations, while not charging fees for personal research, appreciate donations. An increasing number of Record Offices offer to undertake research for a fee. Details are published from time to time in *Family History News and Digest,* but for current information it is best to check direct with Record Offices.

LOCATIONS IN ENGLAND

Barrow Library,Ramsden Square, BARROW IN FURNESS. Cumbria LA14 1LL.
Tel. 01229 870234.
Contact: Local Studies Librarian.
Code: B,C,F,H,L,M,P.

Bedfordshire County Record Office,
County Hall, Cauldwell Street, BEDFORD MK42 9AP. Tel: 01234 228833 Contact: County Archivist. Code B,C,F,H,K,M, P.

Birmingham & Midland Society for Genealogy & Heraldry
Contact:The General Secretary, B&MS for G and H, c/o The Kingsley Norris Room, The Birmingham & Midland Institute, Margaret Street, BIRMINGHAM B3 3BS. The GWR item on page 25 is available on microfiche from the General Secretary on application. Please address postal enquiries to Mr. R. Shakespeare, 303, Eachelhurst Road, Walmley, SUTTON COLDFIELD B76 8DS.

Birmingham Reference Library
Chamberlain Sq. BIRMINGHAM B3 3HQ. Tel: 0121 2354545. Contact Librarian, Social Sciences Dept.

Bishopsgate Institute, 230 Bishopsgate, LONDON EC2M 4QH.
Tel: 0171 247 6844
Contact: Librarian. Code: A,C,G,H,L,M, P.

Brighton Reference Library, Church Street, BRIGHTON BN1 1UE. Contact: Reference Librarian. Code: B,C,G,H,L,M,P

Bristol Central Reference Library, College Green, BRISTOL BS1 Tel: 0117 9299147. Contact: Reference Librarian.
Code:B,C,F, H, L, M, P

Brunel University Library, Cleveland Road, UXBRIDGE, Middx UB8 3PH Tel: 01895 274000 ext 2782. Contact: Librarian. Code: B,C,G,H,L,M,P

Cheshire Record Office, Duke Street, CHESTER CH1 1RL Tel: 01244 602574. Contact: County Archivist.
Code: B,C,E,H,K,M.

Cornwall County Record Office, County Hall, TRURO TR1 3AY Tel: 01872 73698 and 323127. Contact: Duty Archivist.
Code: A,C,E,H,K,M (Sometimes),P.

Coventry City Record Office, Mandela House, Bayley Lane, COVENTRY CV1 5RG. Tel: 01203 25555 Contact: City Archivist.

Cumbria Record Office, 140 Duke Street, BARROW-IN-FURNESS LA14 1XW. Tel: 01229 831269. Contact: Area Archivist. Code: A,C,F,H,L,M,P.

Cumbria Record Office, The Castle, CARLISLE CA3 8UR. Contact: County Archivist. Tel:01228 23456 Ext 2416. Code: B,C,F,H,L,M,P.
A guide to the Cumberland records of some 57 railway companies deposited in the Cumbria Record Office may be purchased from the Record Office. Details on application.

Darlington Railway Centre & Museum, (Ken Hoole Study Centre), North Road Station, DARLINGTON DL3 6ST. Contact: Documentation Officer. Tel 01325 450532. Code: B, C, G, H, L,(Donation appreciated), M. P.

Derbyshire Record Office, County Offices, MATLOCK, DE4 3AG Contact: County Archivist. Tel: 01629 580000 Ext. 7347. Code: A,C,G,H,K,M,P.

Derbyshire Library Service Local Studies, 25b Trongate, DERBY DE1 3GL. Contact: Local Studies Librarian. Tel: 01332 31111 ext 2184. Code: B,C,F,H,L,M,P

Devon Record Office, Castle Street, EXETER EX4 3UP. Contact: County Archivist. Tel: 01392 273509. Code: B,C,E,H,K,M.Q. Note: 48 hours notice required for production of documents as they are out-stored.

Doncaster Central Library, Reference Library, Waterdale, DONCASTER DN1 3JE Tel: 01302 734320. Code: B,C,F,H,L,M,P

Dorset Record Office, County Hall, DORCHESTER DT1 1XS. Contact: County Archivist. Tel: 01305 204414. Code: B, C, G, H, K, M, P

Eastbourne & District Family History Society Contact: Mrs. B.A. Landrock, Walcot, 1 Hindover Crescent, SEAFORD. East Sussex. The LB&SCR item mentioned on page 39 is available by post from Mrs. Landrock. Details on application.

Essex Record Office, County Hall, CHELMSFORD CM1 1LX. Contact: County Archivist. Tel: 01245 267222 ext 2104. Code: B,C,E,H,L,M,P

Greater Manchester County Record Office, 56 Marshall Street, New Cross, MANCHESTER M4 5FU. Contact: County Archivist. Tel: 0161 832 5284. Code: A,C,G,H,K,M.

Great Western Trust, c/o Great Western Society, DIDCOT, Oxon OX11 7NJ. Contact: Trust Secretary. Tel: 01235 817200. Code: D,E,H,L,N,Q

India Office Library and Records, 197 Blackfriars Road, LONDON SE1 8NG. Contact: Enquiries, Catalogue Hall. Tel: 071 928 9531. Code: B,C,F,J,L,M,P

Kent County Library, Ashford Group Library, Church Road, ASHFORD TN23 1QY. Contact: Group Librarian. Tel: 01233 20649. Code: A, C, F, H, L, M, P

Leicester University Library, University Road, LEICESTER LE1 7RH. Contact: Reference Librarian. Code: A,C,G,J

Leicestershire Record Office, 57 New Walk, LEICESTER LE1 7JB. Contact: County Archivist. Tel: 0116 2544566. Code: A,C,F,H,L,M,P

Manchester Central Library, St.Peters Square, MANCHESTER M2 5PD. Contact: Librarian. Tel: 0161 236 9422. Code: B,C,F,H,L,M,Q

National Railway Museum Library, Leeman Road, YORK YO2 4XJ. Contact: Librarian. Tel: 01904 21261. Code:A,C,E,H,L,M,P

Newton Abbot Library, Railway Studies Collection, Bank Street, NEWTON ABBOT TQ12 2RP. Tel: 01626 336128. Contact: Railway Studies Librarian.
Code: B, C, F, L, M, Q.

Northamptonshire Record Office, Delapre Abbey, NORTHAMPTON NN4 9AW. Contact: Chief Archivist. Tel: 01604 62129. Code: B, C, G, H, L, M, P

Nottinghamshire Archive Office, County House, High Pavement, NOTTINGHAM NG1 1HR. Contact: Principal Archivist. Tel: 0115 9504524 Code: B,C,F,H,L,M,Q

Oxfordshire Record Office,
County Hall, New Road,
OXFORD OX1 1ND
Contact: County Archivist
Tel: 01865 815203
Code: B,C,E,H,K,M,P
Note: Fee for postal searches

Public Record Office,
Ruskin Avenue, Kew,
RICHMOND,Surrey TW9 4DU
Contact: Search Dept
Tel: 0181 876 3444
Code: A,C,F,J,L,M,Q

Somerset County Reference Library,
Binford Place, BRIDGWATER TA6 3LF
Contact: Reference Librarian
Tel: 01278 458373
Code: B,C,E,H,L,M,Q
Note: 48 hours required for production of documents as they are out-stored.

Somerset Record Office,
Obridge Road, TAUNTON TA2 7PU
Tel: 01823 87600/78805
Contact: County Archivist

Suffolk Record Office,
St.Andrew House, County Hall,
IPSWICH IP4 2JS
Tel: 01473 55801
Contact: County Archivist
Code: B,C,G,H,K,M,P
Note: Fee for postal searches.

Tyne & Wear Archive Service,
Blandford House, West Blandford Street,
NEWCASTLE-UPON-TYNE NE1 4JA
Tel: 01632 326789
Contact: Search Room
Code: B,C,F,H,L,M,P

Warwick University Library,
COVENTRY CV4 7AL
Tel: 01203 523523 ext 2014
Contact: Librarian Modern Records Centre
Code: B,C,G,H,L,M,Q
Note: As only a minority of railwaymen were union members prior to 1911 any enquiry should include precise information re place of residence.

Widnes Library,
Victoria Road, WIDNES WA8 7QY
Tel; 0151 432 4818
Contact: Area Manager.
Code: B, C, F, H, L, M, P.

Wiltshire County Library Service
Swindon Divisional Library,
Regent Circus, SWINDON SN1 1QG
Tel: 01793 616277
Contact: Reference Librarian
Code: A,C,F,H,L,M,Q

Locations in Scotland

Aberdeen City Libraries,
Rosemount Viaduct,ABERDEEN AB9 1GU
Contact: City Librarian.
Code B,C,F,H,L,M,P

Aberdeen University Library,
Special Collections Dept.,
King's College, ABERDEEN AB9 2UB
Tel: 01224 480241
Contact: Keeper of Special Collections
Code; B,C,F,H,L,M,P

Mitchell Library,
North Street, GLASGOW G3 7DN
Tel: 0141 221 7030
Contact: Departmental Librarian,
Science & Technology Dept
Code: B,C,F,H,L,M,P

Scottish Record Office, HM General Register House, EDINBURGH EH1 3YY Tel: 0131 535 1413. Contact: Officer in charge, West Search Room, West Register House, Charlotte Square,Edinburgh Code: A,C,G,H (limited),L,M,P Note: 24 hours notice required for some outstored documents.

Locations in Wales

Corris Railway Society, Corris Railway Museum, Station Yard, MACHYNLLETH, Powis Contact: Secretary. Code: D,E,H,L,M

Glamorgan Archive Service, County Hall, Cathays Park, CARDIFF CF1 3NE Tel: 01222 820284 Contact: Glamorgan Archivist Code: B,C,F,H,K,M,P Note: Fee for postal searches

Gwent County Record Office, County Hall, Cwmbran NP44 2XH Tel: 0633 832217 or 832266 Contact: County Archivist Code: A, C,G,H,L,M,P

Gwynedd Archives Service, County Offices, CAERNARFON LL54 7EF Tel: 01286 4121 ext 2095 Contact: Area Archivist Code: B,C,F,J,L,M,P

Welsh Industrial and Maritime Museum, Bute Street, CARDIFF CF1 6AN Tel: 01222 481919 Contact: Documentation Officer, Code: B,C,G,H,L,M,P

Locations in Ireland

Public Record Office of Northern Ireland 66 Balmoral Avenue, BELFAST BT9 6NY Tel: 01232 661621 Contact: Dr.Roger Strong Code: A,C,F,H,K,M,P

Irish Railway Record Society, Heuston Station, DUBLIN 8 For Contact details see page 82

Locations in Australia

Australian Archives, ACT Regional Office Cnr Sandford Street and Flemington Road MITCHELL ACT [Postal address:- PO Box 447,BELCONNEN,ACT 2617] Tel: 062 421411 Contact: Assistant Director Access and Information Services Code: Apply for leaflet

State Rail Authority of New South Wales Archives Section,PO Box 29, SYDNEY 2001 Tel: 02 2904907 Contact: Senior Archivist Code: A,C,G,H,K,M,P Note: Postal enquiries not before 1910

Queensland Railway Centre, PO Box 1429, 305,Edward Street, BRISBANE Q 4000 Tel: 225 0211 Contact: Information Officer Code: B,D,E,H,L,M,Q

Australian Archives, South Australian Regional Office, 11-13 Derlanger Avenue, COLLINSWOOD S.A.5081 [Postal address: PO Box 119,WALKERVILLE S.A.5081] Tel: 08 269 3977 Contact: Assistant Director Access and Information Services

Public Record Office of South Australia State Library,North Terrace, ADELAIDE S.A.5000 [Postal address: PO Box 123,Rundle Mall, ADELAIDE S.A.5000] Tel: 223 8793 Contact: Senior Reference Archivist Code: A,C,G,H,L,N,P

Victoria State Transport Authority Secretariat [Level 9] 589 Collins Street, MELBOURNE Vic3000 Tel: 619 4940 Contact: Manager Code: B,C,E,J,L,M,P

Western Australia State Library Service
J.S.Battye Library,
Alexander Library Building,
Perth Cultural Centre, PERTH W.A.6000
Tel: 09 427 3111
Contact:[post] Principal Librarian
     [personal] Enquiry desk
Code: B,C,F,H,L,M,P
Note: 12 hours notice required for
production of some documents as they
are out-stored.

Locations in Canada

BC Rail, PO Box 8770,
VANCOUVER B.C. V6B 4X6
Tel: 604 986 2012
Contact: Personnel Services/Corporate
Library
Code: D,G,H,L,M,P

Provincial Archives of British Columbia
Parliament Buildings, VICTORIA B.C.
Tel: 604 387 1952
Contact: Archivist, Manuscripts and
Govt. Records Division
Code: A,C,F,H,L,M,P

CP Rail Corporate Archives,
PO Box 6042, Station A,
MONTREAL, Quebec H3C 3E4
Contact: Archivist

Locations in Canada (Cont)
Ontario Northland Transportation
Commission Archives,
195 Regina Street,
NORTH BAY, Ontario P1B 8L3
Tel: 705 472 4500 ext 387
Contact: Archivist
Code: B,C,G,H,L,M,Q

Public Archives of Canada.
395 Wellington Street,
OTTAWA, Ontario K1A 0N3
Contact: Archivist, Economic and
Communications Records, Govt
Archives Division
Code: A,C,G,H,L,M,P

Locations in New Zealand
New Zealand Railways
Private Bag,WELLINGTON
Tel: 725599 ext 8738
Contact: Records Manager
Code: B,D,E,H,L,M,P

Locations in United States of America
Union Pacific Railroad,
1416, Dodge Street, OMAHA, Nebraska
68179
Tel: 402 271 3530
Contact: Curator

Locations and contacts in South Africa
See page 85

TROY & BOSTON RAILROAD,

—In connection with—

Western Vermont Railroad,

BENNINGTON ROUTE.
—AND—

Rutland & Washington Railroad,

EAGLE BRIDGE ROUTE.

CARRYING THE UNITED STATES & CANADA MAILS,
AND NATIONAL EXPRESS MATTER TO

TROY, ALBANY, AND NEW YORK.

**No detention by Fog or Low Water between Burlington and
Troy. Meals and Berths unnecessary, makes the
Fare as low as any other Route.**

CONNECTIONS PERFECTLY RELIABLE.

Finding your way around the Public Record Office - a guide for the first time visitor.

Access from Central London is easy by using the Richmond Branch of the District Line, part of the Underground network. Alight at Kew Gardens station, cross the short cul de sac outside and go down West Park Road a few yards. A sign post will direct you left into Burlington Avenue. At its end, across the main road, is Ruskin Avenue at the end of which is the PRO.

There is a different access route for motor vehicles. The PRO is off the A205 Mortlake Road. **If approaching from the Mortlake/Sheen direction**, the entrance is on the right at traffic lights immediately after West Park Avenue, (look out carefully for an AA direction sign). **If coming from Kew Bridge,** the entrance is at traffic lights immediately after Ruskin Avenue, the third turning left after passing under a railway bridge. Again, watch out for an AA sign. Car parking is available and sign posted.

On arrival your bags and briefcases will be checked by security and as you have no reader's ticket you will be directed to the reception desk. Bags and topcoats must be left in the cloakroom and locker area. Fees are returnable, but make sure you have £1 coins with you. Reader's tickets will be provided on the spot on the completion of an application form supported by evidence of identification such as a driving licence or passport. A portion of the application with your signature is used for the reader's ticket which will show your name, number and a barcode. Access to the search and reference rooms is through turnstiles. Wipe the ticket through the barcode reader and the green light indicates you may enter. Go first of all to the Reading Room on the first floor where there are two issue desks covering two groups of workstations. You will be allocated a seat, e.g. desk 25 seat G, and given a bleeper bearing your seat number.

Having done your homework with the directory before coming to Kew you will have with you a list of the items you wish to see, and the next thing is to order them. The instructions for this are given in **Appendix B** and the terminals are in the adjacent Reference Room. If you get into difficulties the staff at the Enquiry desk will be pleased to help. Searches involving staff records less than 75 years old are subject to an undertaking which must be signed at the desk in the Reference Room. In practice, for operational reasons, readers wishing to look at staff records of any age are asked to complete the undertaking and this must be done before the computer will accept the order. The undertaking states:

As a condition of being allowed access to Staff Records not normally made available to the public, I hereby undertake that I will not copy or extract, or publish or communicate with any other person, any information contained in these records other than:

1. the dates of birth, death and service , and

2. details of grade and place of employment of......

While waiting for your items to be processed you can go back to your seat or have a refreshment downstairs, but take your bleeper with you as the issue staff will call you when your items are available. You can then collect one item at a time from the issue desk. Ballpoint and fountain pens are not allowed, so have with you a supply of pencils. Sharpeners are provided outside the Reading Room.

Mention was made on page 7 that information can also be obtained from documents other than staff records, e.g. Board minutes, Board of Trade Accident Reports, etc for which no references are given in this directory. To find these it will be necessary to examine the Class Lists which are held in the Reference Room. Guidance on identifying the documents you want to see is given in General Information leaflet 2, and for convenience the essential elements are quoted here:

> *Leaflets and guides identify classes of records by 'group letters' and 'class numbers'. You need to refer to the CLASS LIST in order to find the number of the 'piece' (that is, the volume or file) you want. There are two sets of Class Lists in the Reference Room and one in the Lobby. Each set runs in alphanumeric order of group letters and class numbers from AB 1 to ZSPC 11. When you find the list of the class you want, it will normally have the piece numbers in the left-hand column, with dates and descriptions of the pieces on the right. (If there are special difficulties about a class list it should have a note at the front explaining how to use it). When you have decided which piece you want to see, you are ready to order.*

If you still have difficulty ask the staff at the Enquiry Desk. You now proceed as set out in **Appendix B**.

When you have finished, return the last item and the bleeper to the issue desk and inform them that you have finished. To get out through the turnstiles you wipe your reader's ticket through the barcode reader.

Now that you have a reader's ticket you can order up to three items in advance by post, telephone or in person, not later than 4.15pm on the day before they are required. These will be available for you when you are allocated a seat in the Reading Room.

Ordering Documents at the Public Record Office, Kew by Computer

ONLY THREE DOCUMENTS MAY BE ORDERED AT A TIME

TO ORDER YOUR DOCUMENTS YOU WILL NEED:

- your reader's ticket and its barcode;
- your location, i.e. your seat number which is also given on your bleeper,
- a full document reference;
- to follow the instructions which appear on screen.

HOW TO ORDER YOUR DOCUMENTS

1. Pass your reader's ticket through the slot in the barcode reader in front of the computer. The barcode reader will show you which way in to place your ticket. If your ticket is not accepted by the system please follow the instructions and enquire at the Reference Desk.

2. When your ticket is accepted by the system, type in your location (seat number). PRESS THE GREEN KEY TO CONTINUE.

3. If you have already used the computer today you will be asked to confirm your location. If you are still using the same seat PRESS THE GREEN KEY TO CONTINUE. If not PRESS THE YELLOW KEY to enter a new location. Type in the new location and press the GREEN KEY to continue.

4. You will now see the document ordering screen

Lettercode	Class	Piece Reference
Enter the Lettercode and then press the GREEN key. Use the BLUE key to correct any typing mistakes. Press the YELLOW key to leave the system.		

Now type in your reference. An example of how the reference should be typed in is given below. **Remember to press the GREEN KEY after typing in each part of the reference.**

Lettercode	Class	Piece Reference
Rail	410	1801

5.   The screen will tell you if your document has been ordered. The references of the documents you have ordered will be displayed at the base of the screen. You will now be asked if you wish to continue ordering. If the answer is yes, PRESS THE GREEN KEY. If no, PRESS THE YELLOW KEY to leave the system.

You will now be asked if you wish to continue ordering from the same class (if you have decided to continue ordering). If you do, PRESS THE GREEN KEY and type in the number of the next piece that you require. If you wish to order documents from a different class, PRESS THE YELLOW KEY and type in the lettercode, class and piece number as described in 4.

6.   The screen will tell you when you have ordered three documents. PRESS THE YELLOW KEY to leave the system.

Your documents have now been ordered and you will be 'bleeped' when they are ready to be collected from the Repository counter.

WHAT TO DO IF YOU MAKE A MISTAKE

The computer will tell you if you have entered any references incorrectly and what you need to do to amend them. Remember to follow the instructions on the screen and use:

- the GREEN KEY to try again,
- the BLUE KEY to correct typing mistakes,
- the YELLOW KEY to leave the system.

PLEASE READ THE INSTRUCTIONS GIVEN ON THE SCREEN CAREFULLY.

IF YOU DO HAVE ANY DIFFICULTIES PLEASE ASK FOR ASSISTANCE FROM STAFF AT THE REFERENCE DESK, GIVING THE MESSAGE ON THE SCREEN AS ACCURATELY AS POSSIBLE.
****

This information has been reprinted from General Information Sheet 29 dated February 1994 with the kind permission of the Public Record Office.

William Catton, Station Master St. Columb Road
and his testimonial volume

One of the hazards experienced by researchers in any Record Office is the ease with which one can be distracted by the variety of material. Such distraction can also produce pleasure when interesting stories are revealed behind the bald entry in an index. This Appendix is included as an example of such a distraction.

As a Cornish railwayman, while trawling through the indexes at Kew for this directory, I kept a lookout for anything with a Cornish flavour, and was intrigued and diverted by the following item in the Great Western Railway lists, Rail 253, piece 508: *Testimonial volume to William Catton, Station Master St. Columb Road. 1906.* Round about that period illuminated testimonials and testimonial volumes were frequently presented to railway staff on their retirement, particularly if subscriptions to a parting gift came from members of the public as well as colleagues, and, if, as seemed likely, it was a retirement testimonial, Mr. Catton must have started his railway career in the mid-1800's, and this was worth investigating.

The railways of mid-Cornwall originated in the 1840's through the enterprise of Squire Treffry of Place, Fowey, to exploit the minerals on his property. He built a private railway connected to the harbour at Newquay on the north coast, and a separate railway connected to his canal and harbour at Par on the south coast. Further railway schemes in the area were projected following his death.

Financial and other problems brought about amalgamations which resulted in the formation of the Cornwall Minerals Railway and a scheme which, among other things, proposed linking Treffry's Newquay and Par railways and extending from Par to Fowey, giving access from Newquay to the main line at Par and to the deep water harbour at Fowey. The line from Fowey to Newquay was opened throughout on 1st June 1874.

One of the stations on the new section between Par and Newquay was called Halloon, subsequently renamed St. Columb Road, and on opening day William Catton, aged 18, resplendent no doubt in his uniform of green serge with brass buttons bearing the CMR monogram, joined the staff of the Cornwall Minerals Railway to take charge of Halloon station as Station Inspector.

Finance became a problem for the Company caused by falling revenue due to reductions in mining output, and a meagre passenger business (it was to be some years before Newquay developed as a seaside resort) and the CMR was forced to ask the Great Western Railway in 1877 to operate the lines on their behalf. In 1896 the GWR bought the lines and with them took over the staff, including William who remained at St. Columb Road, redesignated Station Master. He stayed there for 32 years until June 1906 when he was transferred to Praze on the Gwinear Road to Helston branch in West Cornwall. It was on the occasion of this removal that the testimonial volume was presented to him.

Although St. Columb Road was only a small country station, William's position as Station Master would have given him a respected status in the community. Station Masters in those days were generally involved in local affairs, frequently serving on local Councils. He would have been well known to the passengers, traders and farmers with whom he came into daily contact, and there is no doubting the esteem and regard in which he was held by the local community which he served, as he received a send-off more appropriate to someone retiring after years of faithful service rather than someone moving to another appointment.

The testimonial itself is a handsome volume, with leather binding and all edges gilt, about 10" by 12", with six heavy board pages. It is still in its original box, supplied by W. Crapp, Bookseller and Stationer, St. Columb. The first page is inscribed *Presented to William Catton by his friends of St. Columb and district on his leaving St. Columb Road after occupying the post of stationmaster 32 years. June 1906*, and is a beautiful example of calligraphy and decoration in yellow, orange, green and black. The other five pages list the names of the 182 subscribers, covering a wide spectrum of local gentry, merchants and the general public as well as his railway colleagues. One subscriber described herself simply as 'The Rev. Mother', another as 'A Friend'.

Two cuttings from local newspapers accompany the volume and these describe the presentation arranged one evening at the Indian Queens Working Men's Club and Reading Room, before his departure for West Cornwall. This included a musical entertainment provided by friends from the surrounding villages and eulogistic speeches in which the speakers hoped that when Mr. Catton retired, he and Mrs. Catton would come back to the neighbourhood and renew their acquaintances. Presumably they did not expect to see him back before then. A member of the Cornwall County Council presented William with the volume, a purse of gold and a handsome silver kettle with lamp and stand (the kettle bearing the same inscription as the title page).

In fact he returned sooner than they expected. Eighteen months after saying goodbye he was back on the Par to Newquay branch as Station Master at Luxulyan, three stations away from St. Columb Road, and he remained there until he retired in 1921 at the age of 65.

The Great Western Railway Magazine carried no report of the presentation at Indian Queens, probably for the simple reason that no one sent in the details to the Editor, although in the Staff Changes list it mentioned the transfer to Praze. The transfer back to Luxulyan appears to have been part of a musical chairs arrangement. William went from Praze to Luxulyan. The Luxulyan man went to Perranwell on the Truro to Falmouth branch, and the Perranwell man went to Praze.

Sadly there is also no record of whether William had a retirement presentation when he left the service in 1921. It is most unlikely that after 13 years at Luxulyan and a total of 47 years service he left without some form of recognition, but again this was probably due to no report being send to the Magazine Editor.

Handling the testimonial volume in the quiet atmosphere of Kew I could not help wondering what was passing through William's mind as he accepted it from his friends in the Working Men's Club, and what his reaction would have been if he could have known that it would form part of our national archives. It is a fine example of the social attitudes of the time and has survived by being presented to the British Railways Historical Records in 1966 by Mr. Kinsman, Mayor of Bodmin, and transferred to the custody of the Public Record Office in 1972.

I had hoped that the correspondence which undoubtedly accompanied the gift and would have explained how it came into Mr. Kinsman's possession, would have been with the book. Unfortunately it is not. It is a pity also that it was not accompanied by an account by William of his experiences during those 47 years which spanned an interesting period in the development and expansion of the railway system in Cornwall. Such an account would be invaluable to the present-day railway historian.

Station Masters no longer attend the trains on the platforms at St. Columb Road or Luxulyan, and although the stations themselves have survived so far, their future is less certain than that of William Catton's testimonial volume. The Working Men's Club has undergone conversion.The purse of gold has long since been disbursed, but where, I wonder, is the handsome silver kettle with its lamp and stand?

ABBREVIATIONS

accts - accounts
add - additional
agt - agreement
amalg - amalgamated
app - apprentice
appln - application
appt - appointment
A.S.E. - authorised staff
    establishment
asst - assistant
att - attendance
auth - authorised
bk - book
C. - Carriage (dept)
C&D - collection and delivery
C.M.E. - Chief Mechanical
    Engineer
cen - century
cert - certificate
Ch - Chief
comp - compared
compn - competition
cont - continued
Coy - Company
dept - department
Dist - District
Div - Division/Divisional
D.S.O. - District/Divisional Supt's
    Office
D.T.S. - District Traffic Supt
Engr - Engineer
Elec Engr - Electrical Engineer
G.Mgr - General Manager
inc - including
Insp - Inspector

jnt - joint
L. - Locomotive (dept)
L.C.D. - Locomotive & Carriage
    dept
L.C.& W.D. - Locomotive,
    Carriage & Wagon dept
L.D.C. - Local Departmental
    Committee
M.I.C. - Mutual Improvement
    Class
mins - minutes
misc - miscellaneous
Mtce - Maintenance
ND - no date
Optg - Operating (dept)
proms - promotions
reg - register
sal - salaried
S.C. - Sectional Council
sec - section
Sig - Signal (dept)
S.M. - Station Master
S.O.L. - Superintendent of the
    Line
spl - special
stn - station
super - superannuation
Supt - Superintendent
T.A. - Traffic Apprentice
tfrs - transfers
wkly - weekly
vacs - vacancies

NATIONAL UNION OF RAILWAYMEN

No. 2.

UNITY HOUSE, EUSTON ROAD, N.W.1.

General Secretary :	President :	Assistant General Secretary :
C. T. CRAMP.	W. DOBBIE.	J. MARCHBANK.

To ALL RAILWAY WORKERS

The Railway Companies want to DEDUCT

2s. OUT of EVERY £ You Earn

and they want it from EVERY ONE OF YOU

SIGNALMEN AND SUPERVISORS.
SHOPMEN AND STATION MASTERS.
CLERKS AND CARMEN.
PORTERS & PERMANENTWAY MEN.
CROSSING KEEPERS & CLEANERS.
LOCOMOTIVE MEN AND LOADERS.

Men with Uniform and men without.
Whether you work by Hand or Brain—or both. No distinctions are made. *THEY WANT—*

☞ 2s. IN EVERY £, ☜

and they want it from EACH AND EVERY ONE of you.

IN THE OPINION OF THE TRADE UNIONS THERE IS ONLY ONE REPLY—

NO FURTHER SACRIFICE IS POSSIBLE.

What is *YOUR* view ? It will not be sufficient to express yourself to your family, your friends or your workmates.

Do that, BUT—

TO BE EFFECTIVE YOU MUST ATTEND THE MEETINGS ARRANGED BY YOUR BRANCH.

SPEAK—and ACT, in an ORGANISED MANNER Do it *NOW*.

The "RAILWAY REVIEW" will contain full details of the activities of the Union each week.

October, 1932]

The Co-operative Printing Society Limited, Tudor Street London E.C.4.—45030

To Stop, is shewn by holding **both arms** above the head, thus — or by a **Red Flag**, or by the **violent waving** of any object.

Extract from GWR rule book 1865